BON APPÉTIT!

BONE
APPÉTIT!

GOURMET
COOKING
FOR YOUR
DOG

BY SUZAN ANSON
Illustrated by Bunny Matthews

NEW CHAPTER PRESS, INC.
NEW YORK

Library of Congress Catalog Card Number: 88-60799

ISBN· 0-942257-13 8

Editor: Judy Knipe
Cover and book design: Barbara Marks
Illustrations: Bunny Matthews

For

Emily

and

Raku

ACKNOWLEDGMENTS

I would like to thank Dr. Russell Petro, Dr. Susan Petro and Dr. Regina Schwabe for their careful review of the manuscript and professional suggestions. I would also like to thank Dr. Ben E. Sheffy, Paspari Professor of Nutrition, the James A. Baker Institute for Animal Health, the New York State College of Veterinary Medicine at Cornell University, Chairperson of the National Research Council's Subcommittee on Dog Nutrition for up-to-date information on labeling practices in the commercial dog food industry. Thanks to Sue Hamlin, of the James A. Baker Institute for Animal Health, for her help in providing Dr. Sheffy's tables on canine nutrition. I would also like to thank National Academy Press for making their nutritional charts available (*Nutrient Requirements of Dogs, Revised 1985.*) © 1985 National Academy of Sciences.

I'm, grateful for the friends who contributed recipes, dog stories and support: Joseph Adams, my son Rory Anson, Maryanne Furedi, Erin Martin, Sue Hadley, Harriette Podhoretz, and Richard Raderman.

This project would have been impossible without my husband, John Kirkley, who not only provides a nurturing environment for the dogs and me, but is always there for consultation, support, and technical assistance.

Special thanks go to Judy Knipe for translating the dog recipes into proper cookbook form. And last, but certainly not least, my inspiration and taste-testing crew: Emily, Raku and Jezebel, for their doggie joy and boundless enthusiasm for new tastes.

CONTENTS

PREFACE

The idea for *Bone Appétit!* came to me several years ago when we began restoring our newly acquired house, a distressed, rambling Victorian. At that time, our household consisted of two adults, one teen-age boy, two cats, and Emily and Raku, two middle-aged whippets. The cats, hardy souls, adapted immediately to the new environment. But Emily, a sensitive dog, was off her food, upset by the trauma of the move into a distressed house, bombarded by the noise of workmen, rock 'n roll music, and a constant stream of adolescent boys emulating rock heroes with their own guitars.

I set out to soothe Emily. At mealtime she stood patiently in the red, chartreuse, and yellow kitchen with its greasy cabinets and gazed blankly at the giant peonies on the wet-look vinyl wallpaper. I hoped her lack of appetite wasn't related to the aesthetics of the room. I opened a can of dog food, trying to hide my disgust as its smell permeated the kitchen. Stirring the pasty mush from the can into some packaged kibble, I coaxed, "Atta girl, good Em, here's your dinner . . . mmmmmmmmm . . . good girl. *Good girl.*"

Her chocolate-brown eyes darted nervously at the food, then back to me, then back to the food. She turned and padded quietly out of the kitchen. Once again, I was left, frustrated, with another uneaten dish of top-of-the-line dog food. We both grew thinner.

It was a joke in the family. "But Mom, they hate everything," my son said. At the pet supply store my husband bought every canned and packaged dog food available, and we set them out for Em in an amazing number of permutations and combinations—without success. Maybe this is the wrong approach, we reasoned, and we bought bottom-of-the-line dog food that smelled so terrible we had to evacuate the kitchen while it sat uneaten.

We weighed the arguments of the hard-line behaviorists:

1. Let 'em starve, i.e., when a dog won't eat it's because the owner had no self-discipline. When the dog gets hungry enough, it will eat.
2. Dogs love monotony. If you give the dog table scraps, it will become spoiled and its digestion will be ruined.

Meanwhile, Emily, never robust, became reedier, her ribs prominent, her haunches exposed. This old dog had been with me for over twelve years, and I resolved that I was not going to let her starve herself to death. I decided to cook for her.

Fully aware that she could become an insatiable monster with a predilection for expensive delicacies, one day I would experiment with zucchini and oyster sauce over kibble; the next, fried eggs, rice, and chicken. Success! Emily eagerly awaited each day's new fare. She brightened up, gained weight, and exhibited her old doggie *joie de vivre*.

One afternoon one of the house painters who seemed to have taken up residence with us came into the kitchen. "What are you cooking?" he asked. "It smells great!"

I paused, realizing that if I told him for whom the food was intended I wasn't going to sound sane. Finally I admitted, "I'm cooking for my dog."

"Cooking for your dog?" he roared.

"Yes," I said more firmly, "cooking for my dog."

He had a good laugh, but my embarrassment fueled my imagination. That night I dreamed that I was the owner of the first four-star dog restaurant. When I woke up, Emily was licking my face. It was time for breakfast.

SUZAN ANSON
Warwick, New York
September 1988

INTRODUCTION

Let's spoil our dogs sometimes;
then we shall all be happy.
—Barbara Woodhouse

The first dogs were foragers, digging in early man's scrap piles, hunting for their food. It is only in this century that prepackaged dog food has been available. The implications are startling: Dogs managed to survive as domesticated animals for at least eight thousand years without canned food, kibble, and rubbery nuggets in foil packets. Yet today most of us assume that commercial food is not just preferable, it is essential.

How did we lose all confidence in our ability to feed our animals "people food," or wholesome table scraps and leftovers? Not surprisingly, as packaged dog food was made available, consumers were thrilled to find that they could feed their pets easily and conveniently, a boon for households where everyone was always going off to work. The manufacturers also knew they had to convince the public that their food was indeed balanced and nutritious for all dogs. As the dog food industry grew, it created and promoted a new myth: Unless a dog is fed commercial dog food, it will not thrive and grow; it will, in fact, be in danger of suffering from malnutrition.

The campaign worked. Gradually, dog owners came to feel that they were incompetent to provide a balanced diet for their pets unless it included packaged dog food. Most people are actually afraid to feed their dogs freshly prepared food—the same food they feed themselves and their children.

But there is a minirevolution in the works because health-conscious consumers are starting to figure out that commercial food might be nutritionally inadequate (see appendix). Naturally, the dog food industry has an answer: "upscale" dog food—that is, new packaging and marketing schemes. These are designed to fatten their profits while they still sell you the same old stuff (with, perhaps, some vitamins added). The packaging is more expensive, promising healthier rations well seasoned with snob appeal, and the rallying cries of every pet food commercial are now "gourmet" and "premium."

Not only is the concept of upscale canned pet food ridiculous, it also implies that the canned food previously available was substandard. "Gourmet" dog food from a can is about as creative as canned cranberries and Spam at Thanksgiving dinner.

Nevertheless, despite a growing awareness that commercial dog food is less than nutritionally perfect, consumers who buy only the freshest foodstuffs for the family and who rigorously eschew "human" foods with additives and preservatives do not think twice about loading up the cart with canned dog food. Imagine your family's reaction if you suddenly began to serve only canned food and sugary breakfast cereal at every meal!

It's ironic that as more and more of us acknowledge the dangers of preservatives, additives, toxic sprays, and the antibiotic and hormonal supplements fed to livestock, we nevertheless are instructed that the same old monotonous commercial dog food we feed our pets has been upgraded by the addition of a few vitamins. Given that most of us already have hectic schedules, the convenience of opening a can is very appealing. But are we really doing the best for our pets?

Many veterinarians are convinced that a good per- centage of modern dog maladies stem from a diet of commercial dog food. They cite allergies, kidney disorders, dull coats, and skin problems.

Of course, there are some reputable dog food manufacturers who produce excellent food. Still, there are many, too, who provide only minimal basic nutrition in food that is loaded with fillers and preservatives. A dog rummaging in the garbage cans behind a good restaurant will fare better.

So please ignore those insidious dog food commercials. Think of that smelly, sticky gunk clinging to your own fork! *Not* very appetizing. Think of your beloved pet and how it will thrive if provided with nutritious food. Gather up your courage, learn a few basic principles, and explore the world of gourmet canine cuisine.

Tales of Dogs and Men

The dog, cat, raccoon, weasel, hyena, and bear all have a common ancestor, the Miacis, a carnivore that flourished over fifty million years ago. After another fifteen million years of evolution, the Cynodictis, considered to be the true great-grandfather of the dog, emerged. Among the cynodictis were about forty different doglike creatures, some of them quite startling combinations: There were catlike dogs, bearlike dogs, and hyenalike dogs.

The real dog came into its own five to seven million years ago as a wolflike creature that walked on its toes and was well adapted to hunt and catch prey. A scant million years ago the early wolf roamed Eurasia, and it is this wolf that many experts believe is the direct ancestor of today's dogs and wolves.

Although no one is sure how it happened, about 12,000 years ago certain wolves became domesticated through socialization and breeding, and they developed into dogs. As human beings formed permanent settlements and began to raise crops, dogs were included in village life and used for herding and assisting in the hunt.

Two types of dogs developed fairly early on: companion and worker dogs and those raised as a food source. Today there are over 300 breeds of dog, about 200 of them officially recognized by most major international dog associations. Of these, about 100 are "common," and only about fifty breeds can be considered popular.

The great diversity we see among breeds today is the result of 4,000 generations of breeding—beginning about 8,000 B.C.

In Denmark, 10,000-year-old domestic dog teeth have been found in archaeological excavations that show humans were carefully selecting smaller-jawed animals and breeding them.

Archaeologists in Jarmo, Iraq, found the first representations of dogs in small figures fashioned out of clay. Some of these statuettes have curly tails or show short-statured dogs, traits that were most likely bred into the dogs to distinguish them from wolves.

Numerous breeds of dogs are depicted in Egyptian tomb art, including some resembling greyhounds. Dogs mummies have been discovered in Egyptian tombs, indicating that dogs were probably kept as pets and considered valuable enough to accompany their masters into the afterlife.

An entire dog cemetery, containing the individual graves of about 120 dogs and dating from about 500 B.C., has been discovered in Ashkelon, Israel, about 30 miles south of Tel Aviv. These dogs are believed to have been the hunting hounds of the Persian and Phoenician nobility.

The Romans developed a number of pure breeds throughout their empire, among them dachshunds, salukis, sled dogs (in Viking territory), terriers, and lap dogs. Mastifflike dogs, ancestors of the St. Bernard and great Dane, accompanied the Romans as they crossed the Alps.

In China, it was customary to eat mongrel pups at their tender peak just as they reached maturity. Dog fur was valued too, and the animals were raised for their pelts. As part of their dowry, Chinese brides were given breeding stock of long-haired dogs. Toy dogs were bred to be companions to nobility as recently as 1,000 years ago: These stunted creatures, "sleeve dogs," were refined into the pekingese, pug, and lhasa apso. At about the same time, toys, such as the Italian greyhound, were also appearing in other parts of the world.

Dogs probably came to North America across the Bering Strait from Asia. The earliest remains of the first domesticated North American dog are located at the archaeological site at Jaguar Cave in Birch Creek Valley, Idaho, and have been dated to 10,500 to 8,300 B.C.

In the course of their life among men and because of generations of intensely selective breeding, different kinds of dogs evolved highly specialized sense organs. Among the sighthounds, whose strong suit is their ability to see objects in the far distance, are the greyhound, afghan, saluki, and whippet. Scenthounds, those intrepid trackers of men and game and explosives and drugs, are characterized by their highly developed sense of smell. Some of the best known scenthounds are the bloodhound, basset, and golden retriever.

BASIC FACTS ABOUT DOG NUTRITION

Qualitatively, the dog requires
essentially the same nutriments as man.
—AMERICAN KENNEL CLUB COMPLETE DOG BOOK

A dog's appetite and nutritional needs constantly change throughout his life, much as ours do. Age, activity level, environment, temperament, sickness, and reproductive cycle all play a role.

Wild dogs, like their coyote ancestors, are hunters and depend on freshly killed meat as a food source. But it's interesting to note which part of the animal the wild dog consumes: It goes for the soft meat of the belly first, eating the insides—the organs and intestines. Since most of his prey have a vegetarian diet, the dog consumes a fair amount of vegetation along with the meat. So, although they are carnivorous, all dogs must have what would be considered, in human terms, a well-balanced diet. Eating meat exclusively can cause what many veterinarians refer to as "all-meat syndrome," a dangerous imbalance in the calcium and phosphorous ratios of the diet. This syndrome can cause joint diseases, fragile bones that break under the dog's own weight, weight loss, diarrhea, and a dull coat.

In fact, dogs need the same nutrients as we do—protein, fat, and carbohydrates—and they need them in roughly the same percentages of total daily calorie intake:

Recommended Content of Dog Foods

	Non-working Adult	Young Adult Pregnant Bitch Working or Stressed Adult	Puppy or Lactating Bitch
Protein*	16%	20%	24%
Fat	10%	12%	14%
Carbohydrate	44%	38%	32%
Calories from protein	20%	24%	28%
Vitamins and Minerals	A	B	C

*Values are for high-quality protein. For average-quality protein, add two or three percentage points.

A. Values recommended by the National Research Council.
B. Values as for A plus 10%.
C. Values as for A plus 20%.

Chart courtesy of Dr. Ben E. Sheffy, James A. Baker Institute for Animal Health, Cornell University.

Protein

Protein, which is essential in every dog's diet, provides about 25 amino acids necessary for the growth, repair, and maintenance of healthy muscles, bones, and internal organs. Experts say that between 15 and 30 percent of the total calories in a dog's diet should be protein. The National Research Council is an agency of the National Academy of Sciences with responsibility for setting nutritional guidelines for minimum nutrient requirements for growth, reproduction, lactation, and muscular activity for pets and their human owners. According to the National Research Council, protein requirements are influenced by digestibility, caloric density in the diet, the physiology of the dog, and the composition of amino acids in the diet.*

Dogs digest about 90 percent of the eggs and meat they consume, but only 60 to 80 percent of vegetable protein. In the scheme of dog digestion, wheat gluten and cooked kidney beans, for instance, are only half as digestible as meat.

Raw and Cooked Meats. Raw meat is hazardous in your dog's diet. Uncooked meat can harbor parasites, bacteria, and viruses. Dogs have strong stomachs and they're capable of digesting things that humans can't, but if foods are contaminated with bacteria, food poisoning can result. Puppies can die from consuming tainted food. Meats should be cooked to destroy parasites that may be present,

*from NRC *Nutrient Requirements of Dogs,* Revised 1985 © 1985. National Academy Press. National Academy of Sciences.

such as trichinosis organisms and worms. Poultry should also be well cooked to prevent any salmonella organisms from polluting the food.

Use a variety of meats, including organ meats. Dogs love liver, and it is recommended by many breeders. But since liver stores many toxic substances and pollutants, it should be rotated in the diet and used only occasionally.

Eggs. The egg is one of nature's most perfect foods. Raw eggs were a favorite of my dog Emily before she left her country home. The same impulse that led her to raid the chicken coop guides many wild predators. However, scientific studies indicate that raw egg whites can cause a biotin deficiency, which in turn can lead to problems with a dog's nervous system and with its coat, as well. Even though it would take a large number of raw eggs over time to create an imbalance, it's best to err on the side of safety and cook the eggs. Dogs love them scrambled, poached, and fried.

Milk. After puppies are weaned, most veterinarians recommend that milk be removed from the diet on the assumption that the pup will gain necessary nutrients from other foods. Some dogs are lactose intolerant; that is, they are unable to digest milk properly and may suffer from intestinal gas and diarrhea. Since many farm dogs thrive on cow's milk, apparently never developing an intolerance, it is possible that pasteurization may be the culprit, since it changes the chemical structure of the milk and destroys enzymes and bacteria. If you want to include milk in your dog's diet, try raw milk and goat's milk. The lactose in cultured milk products has been altered by bacteria, so yogurt, buttermilk, and cheese are usually well tolerated.

Fats

Fats are a highly concentrated source of energy. Most commercial dog foods contain between 4 and 10 percent fat, but your dog may require up to 30 percent fat in his diet for optimum energy. Fats are necessary to maintain a healthy coat and skin and to keep the nervous system in good working order. Fat is 100 percent digestible, and it increases the palatability of most other food. Dogs whose protein intake is restricted can obtain energy through fat in the diet while still reducing the strain on the liver and kidneys.

Carbohydrates

The primary source of energy, carbohydrates can provide up to 60 percent of a dog's daily calories. High-level complex carbohydrates (polysaccharides), which are the kind you want to feed your dog, are present in wheat and grain products, rice, potatoes, and other starchy vegetables (dried legumes, such as beans and lentils). Simple carbohydrates include sucrose (sugar) and lactose (milk sugar).

Vitamins and Minerals

Vitamins are essential to your dog's growth and well-being. If you have any uncertainties about the proper levels for your pet, consult your veterinarian. Curiously, unlike humans, dogs are able to manufacture their own vitamin C. However, many experts believe that large breeds cannot supply enough of this vitamin naturally, and recommend that you give your dog vitamin C supplements.

Minerals work with vitamins to form important enzymes necessary to support life. The National Research Council has published specific guidelines for certain minerals: calcium, phosphorous, potassium, magnesium, manganese, iron, copper, iodine, zinc, sodium, and selenium.

Sodium. Dogs need salt to maintain proper fluid balance and avoid water retention or dehydration. A dog with heart disease is usually placed on a low-sodium diet. If your dog is eating a well-balanced diet, there is no need for table salt to be added. *Bone Appétit!* recipes call for salt to taste, which means just the tiniest pinch to enhance the natural flavors of the food.

Minimum Nutrient Requirements of Dogs for Growth and Maintenance
(amounts per kg of body weight per day)[a]

Nutrient	Unit	Growth[b]	Adult Maintenance[c]	Nutrient	Unit	Growth[b]	Adult Maintenance[c]
Fat	g	2.7	1.0	**Minerals**			
Linoleic acid	mg	540	200	Iron	mg	1.74	0.65
Protein[d]				Copper	mg	0.16	0.06
Arginine	mg	274	21	Manganese	mg	0.28	0.10
Histidine	mg	98	22	Zinc	mg	1.94	0.72
Isoleucine	mg	196	48	Iodine	mg	0.032	0.012
Leucine	mg	318	84	Selenium	µg	6.0	2.2
Lysine	mg	280	50	**Vitamins**			
Methionine-cystine	mg	212	30	A	IU	202	75
Phenylalanine-				D	IU	22	8
tyrosine	mg	390	86	E[e]	IU	1.2	0.5
Threonine	mg	254	44	K[f]			
Tryptophan	mg	82	13	Thiamin	µg	54	20
Valine	mg	210	60	Riboflavin	µg	100	50
Dispensable amino				Pantothenic acid	µg	400	200
acids	mg	3,414	1,266	Niacin	µg	450	225
Minerals				Pyridoxine	µg	60	22
Calcium	mg	320	119	Folic acid	µg	8	4
Phosphorus	mg	240	89	Biotin[f]			
Potassium	mg	240	89	B_{12}	µg	1.0	0.5
Sodium	mg	30	11	Choline	mg	50	25
Chloride	mg	46	17				
Magnesium	mg	22	8.2				

[a] Needs for other physiological states have not been determined.
[b] Average 3-kg-BW growing Beagle puppy consuming 600 kcal ME/day.
[c] Average 10-kg-BW adult dog consuming 742 kcal ME/day.
[d] Quantity sufficient to supply minimum amounts of available indispensable and dispensable amino acids specified below.
[e] Requirement depends on intake of PUFA and other antioxidants. A fivefold increase may be required under conditions of high PUFA intake.
[f] Dogs have a metabolic requirement, but a dietary requirement was not demonstrated when natural ingredients were fed.

Nutrient Requirements of Dogs, Revised 1985, © 1985 Reprinted courtesy: National Academy of Sciences.

Supplementation. Just as many of us substitute vitamins and minerals, sometimes in very high and/or uneven doses, for well-balanced meals, we may try to "help" our dogs in the same way. If you can't make it home from work until midnight a few nights during the week, you may find yourself feeling sorry for your pet—it's not getting enough attention or exercise, and we won't even mention the pooch's overextended bladder.

But what will assuage some of your guilt? Vitamins, of course! Popping a few vitamins into the dog food may make you feel better, but it's likely to set up metabolic imbalances in your dog unless you really calculate your dog's requirements and determine whether any real deficiencies exist.

Doctors can't agree on supplementation for humans, and canine experts can't reach a consensus either. If you must supplement, consult your veterinarian and get a recommendation for specific supplements and dosage. If you do use a supplement, veterinary formulations are your best bet. Pet-Tabs by Beecham Laboratories are an excellent daily supplement for dogs and cats. Pet-Tabs Plus is formulated for dogs with higher requirements: older dogs, show dogs, and hunting dogs. Pet-Tabs F.A. contains fatty acids and zinc for poor, shedding coats.

Common sense tells us that a varied diet of fresh foods usually meets our own nutritional needs, and the same is true for dogs. The key word is *fresh*. And that, by definition, rules out nearly all commercially processed dog foods.

Fiber

Fiber, popular in the diets of health-conscious dog owners, also contributes to dog health and should comprise about 5 percent of a healthy dog's diet. Good sources of dietary fiber are whole-grain cereals, including bran, and fresh, crunchy vegetables.

A Word about Bones

All dogs love to chew. Bones can provide hours of pleasure and also assist in the removal of tartar from the teeth. The selection of the right bone is important to your pet's well-being. Most bones cannot be chewed without serious side effects. For instance, bone splinters can accumulate in the colon and create severe constipation. Short, round bones can become lodged in the dog's throat or jaw, creating problems that can only be solved surgically.

Safe substitutions include synthetic chewing bones or natural rawhide chews. However, some dogs are sensitive to rawhide and experience vomiting and diarrhea. No matter how large and safe a natural bone may be, a determined dog with a powerful bite can splinter the largest bone. In short, for your dog's safety and well-being, never give your dog a natural bone.

Special Nutritional Needs

Extra Protein. High-protein diets are essential for pregnant dogs, puppies during their first year of rapid growth, and stressed or convalescing dogs. Some commercial kibbles, such as Eukanuba Premium and Nutro Puppy Food, have about 30 percent protein content to meet these increased needs.

Exposure to freezing weather or extreme heat will also increase a dog's need for protein. Extra calories will be required to help dogs maintain weight during the cold season. Dogs who are outdoors all the time or who sleep outdoors will have a higher caloric requirement than the indoor pet.

Pregnant Bitches. Starting with the fifth week of pregnancy, pregnant females should be fed from a third to a half more food than normal, including high-quality protein. As the pregnancy progresses, it is better to feed smaller meals more frequently to keep her comfortable as the puppies grow. You should also administer a vet-prescribed vitamin and mineral supplement.

Orphaned Newborn Pups. Use a commercial formula (KMR or Esbilac) or your own homemade formula for orphaned pups that have not yet been weaned. If you want to make your own puppy formula, combine in a blender 1¼ cups of evaporated milk, ¼ cup of warm water, 2 teaspoons of protein powder, and 2 egg yolks. Blend until smooth and feed to the puppy. Protein powders are available in health food stores, and it's best to use one derived from milk and egg sources (casein, egg albumin, or lactalbumin) in order to supply necessary amino acids. Not all puppies can tolerate cow's milk, and some pups may experience constipation when given milk substitutes.

Young Puppies. By the middle of the third week of life, pups can be introduced to a slurry of milk and baby cereal twice a day. The puppies will take to the new food more readily if you first offer it to them by putting a small amount on your finger and letting them lick it off. Later they can have some mashed grains, packaged puppy growth food, and milk.

Older Dogs. Some dogs live to be twenty, and some live only half that long, but most dogs have a life span of between ten and fifteen years. Many factors influence your

Feeding Tips for Older Dogs

- eliminate foods that are hard to digest: spicy, greasy, or salty foods
- substitute chicken or fish with rice instead of meat and meat byproducts

dog's life span: breed, genetic endowment, and environmental factors, among them food.

DOG YEARS	HUMAN YEARS	DOG YEARS	HUMAN YEARS
1	15	10	56
2	24	11	60
3	28	12	64
4	32	13	68
5	36	14	72
6	40	15	76
7	44	16	80
8	48	17	84
9	52	18	88

—Courtesy Russell Petro, D.V.M.

You can't control your dog's genetic inheritance, but you do have control over nutritional and environmental factors.

Older dogs should have regular checkups to discover or monitor a wide range of geriatric problems. A few of these, such as kidney disorders and weight loss, can be managed to some extent by nutritional means.

Stressed, Ill, and Convalescing Dogs. Dogs who are under stress, whether it be from a recent move, a dog show, family upheaval, or illness, have increased nutritional requirements. A stressed dog may require extra calories as well as temporary increase in vitamin and mineral supplements.

Pet Stress Checklist

- ☐ unhappy owner
- ☐ family conflict
- ☐ tail docking
- ☐ ear clipping
- ☐ surgery
- ☐ recent move
- ☐ vacation
- ☐ new household member
- ☐ loss of household member, including other pets
- ☐ pet ill or disabled
- ☐ new household schedule
- ☐ household upheaval (construction, redecorating)
- ☐ loss of privilege
- ☐ stay in kennel

FEEDING PRACTICES

How Much?

Adult dogs, if left to their own devices, will eat when hungry, eat only enough to be satisfied, and will not overeat or become fat. The question remains, however: How much should you feed your dog? The American Kennel Club cites the old adage, "the eye of the master feeds his dog," and recommends feeding adult dogs once or, preferably, twice a day. How does this translate into caloric intake?

Smaller dogs burn more calories per pound than larger breeds. For example, a 10-pound dog needs about 42 calories for each pound of body weight, while a larger dog (50 to 75 pounds) requires about 26 calories per pound of body weight. Of course a dog's age, condition, lifestyle, and breed will also affect its daily caloric requirement. Equally important, the AKC recommends establishing a feeding schedule and sticking to it.

Puppies need four times as many calories as an adult dog. However, some pet owners unknowingly push their pups nutritionally to bring them to maximum size for their breed. It's best to let the puppy grow at its own rate, since overfeeding can contribute to illnesses in the adult dog.

Climate is a factor in how much your dog needs to eat. In very cold weather, dogs need to consume more food to maintain their weight. In very warm climates, a dog may eat less, but will still require the same amount of protein required in milder climates.

Sick dogs and those recovering from surgery, malnutrition, or illness should be given small amounts of food that will not overwhelm the digestive system, such as rice, chicken, and nutritious broths. Food may be gradually increased to bring the dog up to proper weight.

When?

Some dog owners make dry food available all day, some will feed on demand, but most people are comfortable feeding an adult dog once or twice a day. Routine is comfortable for most of us, and dogs also appreciate consistency in their lives, so feed your dog at the same times and in the same place every day. This constancy will also help regulate the dog's elimination cycle. A dog that hasn't finished eating within thirty minutes has probably had enough. Leftover food should be covered and refrigerated.

Weak puppies may need to be fed separately at two- to three-hour intervals. Special nursing bottles can be obtained from the veterinarian.

Pups from seven to twelve weeks should be fed four times a day. At twelve weeks to six months, young dogs do best on a three-feedings-a-day schedule, and from six months to maturity twice a day is sufficient.

Hunting dogs and those who perform under strenuous conditions (water rescue, coursing, and other activities) will benefit from a twice-a-day feeding schedule.

Between-meal snacks should be discouraged. Snacking can create a begging pattern that is a nuisance and can also contribute to obesity. Once in a while, of course, it's all right to give your dog a small scrap, but it is the spirit in which the snack is given that is important. When offering a tidbit, be sure to make a show of praise so the dog realizes that your love is the most important thing, and the food is just a delightful accompaniment.

Fasting Your Pet

Many veterinarians suggest that occasionally you fast your dog for a day so its system can slough off toxic accumulations. A dog will go off its feed naturally from time to time, and a day without food is a common occurrence in the wild. If your pet is ill and develops a fever, its appetite will naturally decrease—remember the old adage, "starve a fever." During this voluntary or imposed period of fasting, offer your pet nutritious broths, a few light vegetables, and a small amount of lean cooked meat.

Feeding Bowls

Your dog should have its own bowls for food and water. The size, shape, weight, and height of the bowls are factors we usually don't think about, but they are important to your dog.

Some breeds, particularly the larger ones, and dogs who are prone to choke on their food will benefit from a bowl that is raised off the floor.

Long-eared dogs need deep bowls with narrow, contoured openings designed to keep the ears out of the food. Not only is it a chore to clean food residue off a dog's ears, but the food can also create an ear infection.

Plastic and stainless steel bowls are convenient, but they are often too light and end up being pushed across the kitchen floor as your dog eagerly wolfs down its dinner. In addition, some dogs may be sensitive to certain types of plastic and may develop redness or swelling around their mouths. Glazed ceramic bowls, if chipped, may present a lead-poisoning hazard. The best bowl to use is a sturdy ceramic one well-suited to your dog's size and individual characteristics.

Needless to say, a dog's bowl should be washed after each feeding to prevent bacterial growth.

Feeding More Than One Dog

Two dogs competing for the same meal will be in conflict; the dominant dog will usually prevail, but not before snarling and nipping have ensued. I feed my dogs at opposite ends of the kitchen so that each can dine in a leisurely manner without worrying that the other will steal part of its dinner.

A dog will sometimes bite if its feeding area is invaded. For this reason, toddlers and small children should be taught to stay away from the dog while it's eating and never to take anything out of its mouth.

If one of your dogs is on a special diet, it's hard to determine who's getting what if food is eaten from a shared dish. Greedy dogs who eat other dogs' food can become overweight. And if a dog isn't eating because it's sick, who's to know if both bowls are licked clean? When one dog is young and another middle-aged or on a special diet, the food will be different and shouldn't be mixed. In such cases, feed the dogs in separate rooms, if necessary, and always use separate bowls, whether the dogs are on special diets or not.

TROUBLESOME FEEDING ISSUES

Begging

In our culture, food is often equated with love as well as nutrition. It's important to separate the two. We feed dogs because they must eat to sustain life, not because we want their love. It's easy to condition an animal, and if you try to train a dog with goodies, it will respond to food, not to your love. This makes for a dog who will not respond in a consistent manner, a situation that could be life-threatening for him. Dogs naturally associate food with their hunger. Food cannot substitute for fondness, petting, and companionship. It is up to us to understand these distinctions and act on them.

Begging is a difficult habit to break. It's also annoying when you are trying to eat a meal. Clever dogs will play the part to the hilt, begging, whining, and barking, not to mention drooling on you or your guests with anticipation or, worse, taking food from a child. Patterns develop quickly, and you must decide what behavior you're willing to live with. If it's clear to the dog that you're the leader, it will happily fall into line and do its best to please you, otherwise the dog will instinctively try to get control of the situation.

Deciding that food and love are separate doesn't necessarily condemn your dog to a lifetime of dreary dry food.

Bone Appétit! has maintenance recipes suitable for both daily use and occasional treats that can be used sparingly or in combination with the main course.

Fat Dogs

Sadly, it is estimated that in the United States between 30 to 40 percent of dogs are overweight.

Obesity has many side effects that can contribute to the decline of your pet's well-being and vitality. Fat dogs have more ailments and don't live as long. Some of the conditions that may be caused or worsened by your pet's obesity include:

- arthritis
- hip dysplasia
- heart, lung, or liver disease
- diabetes
- pancreatitis
- gastrointestinal problems
- skin disease

Furthermore, if your dog is too heavy, it will be less able to enjoy life. The overweight dog is uncomfortable, and that will tend to make it grouchy. Fat dogs can't exercise well because they've got to lug around all that extra weight. They can't take the heat because they're wearing a coat of blubber under their fur coats. And a fat dog makes more trips to the vet during its life because its resistance is lowered. When an obese dog needs surgery, it is at a higher risk than thinner dogs due to the increased stress on its heart and circulation.

Testing your dog's fat level is easy: With your dog standing, place the palms of your hands over its rib cage on the sides, not on the stomach below. When you run your fingers lightly along the dog's sides, you should be able to feel bone. If you can actually count the ribs as you move your hands along the dog's side, the dog is underweight. If you can't feel anything, try to look objectively at your dog and make an assessment, or ask a neighbor to administer the test for you. It's usually hard to admit that your dog is—let's face it—*fat*, but once you confront the problem, you can proceed with a nutritional plan. Most dog owners are content to weigh their dogs during yearly veterinarian exams. However, it's a good idea to keep a chart of your dog's weight and to make notations on a regular basis, to determine that the quantity of food is in keeping with your goal for the dog.

For the overweight dog, the course of action is clear: Reduce the dog's food intake. Sounds simple, but this is where all your beliefs about what makes the dog happy come into play. In truth, dieting is much simpler for your dog than for you. You're going to assist him because you'll exercise willpower for him. The dog can eat only what you provide and no more. Less food will increase the dog's use of fat stores, and —*voilà!*—thin dog.

However, before you put your dog on a diet, check with your veterinarian to be sure that the regime you've designed is sound. Here are some basic rules:

- Before beginning the diet, consult with your veterinarian to set up a workable reduction plan for your pet
- Enlist the cooperation of your entire family
- Don't feed your pet with other animals while he's dieting
- Divide the dog's food into two or three daily servings
- Be consistent: don't help your dog cheat on the diet— do not feed anything that is not in the program
- Give your dog lettuce if he begs at the table while you're eating
- Decrease intake gradually, unless your veterinarian thinks the dog is in a life-threatening situation and directs otherwise
- Exercise the dog daily—it's good for both of you

What is a reasonable rate of weight reduction? Generally speaking, small dogs can lose up to one pound a week, medium dogs up to two pounds, and large dogs up to three pounds. Most dogs will require two to three months on a diet.

Thin Dogs

While some dogs are too fat, others are too thin. Some even eat enormous amounts of food without absorbing the nutrients. How do you determine if your dog is too thin? Run your fingers lightly over your dog's rib cage. It's fine to just barely feel the ribs, since no fat should cover them, but you shouldn't be able to feel the grooves between each rib. If you can, you'll want to increase your dog's caloric intake. You'll also want to know why your dog is so thin.

Causes of underweight include parasites, disease, and underfeeding. Once the first two factors are either treated or ruled out, you can simply increase your dog's consumption. Try multiple feedings and free feeding—making food available to your pet at all times, so he can munch whenever he's hungry. And, in the same spirit of moderation mentioned earlier, increase quantities gradually. Don't expect to plump up your dog instantly.

Record your dog's starting weight and progress on a chart to make sure that the weight gain is slow and steady. Once your dog approaches the proper weight, you can cut down on the quantities.

Some dogs are unable to absorb the nutrients in their food. One of the obvious signs is a thin dog who has frequent and bulky stools. The food is passing through, but not much gets absorbed. With some poor-quality commercial pet foods, the fillers and low-quality proteins run right through the system, unassimilable by the dog. Often a change of diet will soothe the dog's system. A gentle and easily tolerated meal is a bland chicken and rice casserole (page 123), or perhaps beef broth (page 83) or chicken stock (page 84) with a few vegetables.

Shaping Up

Exercise will energize your pet and take its mind off the deprivation of its diet. Substitute a walk in the woods for that second helping with gravy. Soon the dog will anticipate its walks with you instead of dreaming about chopped liver smothered in chocolate sauce. A fat dog is not in condition, though, so be sure to exercise gently— it's not boot camp. Be sensitive to the dog's level of endurance and don't expect him to become a world-class Frisbee champ overnight. In hot weather, remember that the overweight dog can't tolerate extreme heat and may suffer from heatstroke if the workout is too demanding.

ABOUT THE RECIPES

The recipes in *Bone Appétit!* are based on wholesome, fresh ingredients that you would ordinarily use in preparation for your own "people" cuisine. Most of the ingredients are easily found in the market, and I bet most of the dry ingredients are already in your pantry.

There are, of course, a few ingredients that will stretch your budget: Truffles (Egg and Truffle, page 65) are unquestionably a wild extravagance and certainly not for the fainthearted. Other recipes, particularly in the chapter "Dog Biscuits and Other Snacks," combine the simplest of ingredients: flour, egg, and oil. Some ingredients require more ingenuity: You may have to special order some of the organ meats from the butcher. Items such as charcoal and soy flour can be found at your neighborhood health food store, which you'll find is a great resource for the imaginative dog cook.

Some dishes you will find quite economical and simple to prepare, while others are definitely meant for special occasions and will provide a pleasant way for you and your dog to while away a rainy afternoon.

In my own experience, it is easy to toast up a batch of fresh kibble for the week while preparing my own family's meals. When I'm making Raku's weekly ration, she follows every step I make in the process. In the beginning, I concocted numerous stir-fry dishes for Emily because they were quick and provided a good balance of meat, vegetables, and grain.

Although the recipes vary in their makeup of proteins, fats, and carbohydrates, the ingredients are fresh, additive-free, and packed with nutrients.

Because its nose is highly sensitive, a dog lives in a world of scents that we can only begin to imagine. It is estimated that a dog's nose is a million times more sensitive than the human nose. At any moment, a dog is registering multiple scent trails, one overlaying another, some strong, others faint. Amazingly, dogs are able to differentiate individual odors from this olfactory potpourri; they are equipped with forty times more brain cells devoted to recognizing scents than man. A dog brings all of this native nasal talent to bear in the matter of dinner and will subject its food to the sniff test prior to sampling.

Although the canine's sense of smell will override its taste buds, dogs have certain preferences and dislikes when it comes to taste. Spoiled, gamey foods appears to be a great preference. Most dogs dislike citrus fruits and acidic food, some dogs hate cold food, and they all seem to love sweets.

Bone Appétit! begins with recipes for biscuits and other snacks and finishes with Decadent Doggie Desserts.

Once you begin to cook for your dog, you'll get a sense of how much food it will need. Keep in mind the amount you would ordinarily feed and make adjustments, up or down, accordingly. It's amazingly simple to include a few basic dog recipes in your weekly routine. Once cooked, most of the dishes should be covered well with foil or plastic wrap, then stored in the refrigerator to preserve freshness. Unused portions can be frozen.

Recently, a friend confided that she had panicked during a storm after discovering there was no canned food for her keeshond, Max. Weather prevented her from getting to the store, and she momentarily despaired. She rummaged through the pantry, looking for a stray can of food. As she pushed past the flours, grains, and cereals, she realized she was overlooking the obvious. Oatmeal, eggs, tuna, perhaps in a light tomato sauce. Presto! Max survived and grew to love canine cuisine, and so will all the deserving doggies lucky enough to eat the fruits of your labor.

BONE APPÉTIT!

If you pick up a starving dog and make him prosperous, he will not bite you. This is the principal difference between a dog and a man.
—Mark Twain,
 Puddin'head Wilson

DOG BISCUITS AND OTHER SNACKS

In the late 1800s, James Spratt, an American entrepreneur, found himself in London peddling lightning rods. Sales were few and far between, and Spratt, unable to find appealing food for his canine traveling companion, concocted a mixture of meat, meal, and vegetables, a meal in a cake. His dog received the biscuits with enthusiasm. Spratt, seizing the opportunity, patented what would be sold as Spratt's Meat Fibrine Dog Cakes and started a revolution in prepared dog food.

By the end of the century, English and American manufacturers of dog biscuits were competing fiercely for a share of the market. Some of the claims were extravagant. Spratt's Meat Fibrine Dog Cakes rivaled snake oil as a cure-all and a nutrient. The cakes were salt free, ready to eat, and even, it was asserted, capable of ridding dogs of worms and distemper. The Slater Brothers waged a campaign of testimonials for their product. Lord George Cavendish claimed that Slater's Meat Biscuits were "a great advantage when men and dogs came in after a long day. I have recommended your meat biscuit to several of my friends." The Anchor Biscuit Works of London hit the market with a unique product: W. G. Clarke's Buffalo Meat Biscuits, a trendy import supplied to the Crystal Palace Company for the fussiest dog shows.

In the tradition of these pioneering dog biscuit manufacturers, you may choose to bake your own dog biscuits. Most of the ingredients are available in supermarkets, but for items such as soy flour or oat bran, try a good health food store. Some of these snacks are crunchy, others softer and lighter—your dog will love them all.

BASIC, CRUNCHY, TEETH-CLEANING BISCUITS

1 cup whole wheat flour
1 cup unbleached all-purpose flour
½ cup wheat germ plus additional for dredging biscuits
¼ cup nonfat dry milk powder
1 cup Chicken Stock (page 84)
3 tablespoons corn oil
2 tablespoons chopped parsley
½ teaspoon salt

Preheat oven to 400° F. and oil a large baking sheet.

Combine whole wheat and all-purpose flours, ½ cup wheat germ, the milk powder, and salt. In a small bowl, mix together stock and oil. Put one-third flour mixture in a mixing bowl; add one-third stock mixture and stir until dough is well combined. Continue adding flour and stock mixtures by thirds, stirring until all ingredients are well mixed.

Turn dough out on lightly floured surface and knead well, adding additional all-purpose flour as necessary, until dough is easier to handle, but still soft. Break off walnut-size pieces of dough, roll them in wheat germ, and place on prepared baking sheet about 1 inch apart.

Flatten biscuits with a fork. Bake 15 to 20 minutes, or until fully baked. Turn off heat and allow biscuits to harden in oven for several hours. Store biscuits, covered, in refrigerator or freezer. *Makes about 24 biscuits.*

A dog's teeth are nearly self-cleaning. Although not prone to cavities, they do tend to accumulate tartar. Crunchy dog biscuits and crisp, briefly-cooked fresh vegetables will help prevent tartar formation and keep your dog's teeth bright and shiny.

No one appreciates the very special genius of your conversation as a dog does.
—Christopher Morley

MIXED-GRAIN BISCUITS

One of the nimblest dogs on record was known as Crumstone Danko, a German shepherd who scaled a wall over eleven feet high in a single bound, as we know from *The Guinness Book of World Records*. These biscuits, high in complex carbohydrates, will give your dog a boost, too.

1 cup whole wheat flour
1 cup cornmeal
½ cup nonfat dry milk powder
2 teaspoons baking powder
½ teaspoon salt
¼ cup cold vegetable shortening
1 cup water
½ cup cooked bulgur

Preheat oven to 400° F. and grease a large baking sheet.

Sift flour, cornmeal, milk powder, baking powder, and salt into a mixing bowl. Cut in shortening. Slowly add water, stirring with a fork, until mixture forms a soft dough. Add bulgur and mix well.

Turn dough out on lightly floured surface and knead lightly.

Divide dough in half and roll out one piece into a circle ¼ inch thick. Cut into 9 wedges with a floured knife and place wedges on prepared baking sheet. Repeat with second piece of dough. Bake 15 minutes, or until lightly browned. *Makes 18 biscuits.*

PUPPY-BREATH BISCUITS

2 cups whole wheat flour
½ teaspoon salt
1 tablespoon charcoal (available at health food stores)
1 large egg, lightly beaten
3 tablespoons vegetable oil
½ cup chopped Italian parsley
2 tablespoons chopped fresh mint
⅔ cup milk

Preheat oven to 400° F.

Combine flour, salt, and charcoal. In a medium bowl, combine egg, oil, parsley, and mint; mix well. Slowly stir in flour mixture, then add enough milk to make a dough the consistency of drop biscuits. Drop heaping tablespoons of dough about 1 inch apart onto greased baking sheets. Bake 15 minutes, or until firm and lightly browned.

Store cooled biscuits in tightly covered container in refrigerator. The minty aroma will travel to other foods if biscuits are not well sealed. *Makes about 24 biscuits.*

Did you ever notice how sweet and wonderful a puppy's breath is, but how horrible that of a grown dog can be? The parsley, mint, and charcoal in these biscuits will act as breath sweeteners, and your dog will have almost kissable breath! Charcoal, a human nutritional supplement, can be obtained at health food stores.

FLEA-BANE BISCUITS

They say a reasonable number of fleas is good fer a dog— keeps him from broodin' over bein' a dog.
—Edward Noyes Westcott,
  David Harum

Fleas are the scourge of all dogs, and there are many of us who don't want to resort to chemical sprays and powders. There is evidence that certain natural supplements will make your dog less attractive to fleas and other insects. Brewer's yeast and garlic are the most effective. Brewer's yeast is a great supplement as you can't overdo it and harm the dog. Most dogs initially don't like the flavor, so you must introduce it very slowly. Once your dog becomes accustomed to the taste, you can sprinkle it over everything to build up flea resistance.

2 cups unbleached all-purpose flour
½ cup wheat germ
½ cup brewer's yeast
1 teaspoon salt
2 cloves garlic, minced
3 tablespoons vegetable oil
1 cup Chicken Stock (page 84)

Preheat oven to 400° F. and oil 2 or 3 baking sheets.

Combine flour, wheat germ, brewer's yeast, and salt. In a large mixing bowl, combine garlic and oil. Slowly stir flour mixture and stock alternately into oil and garlic, beating well, until the dough is well mixed.

Shape dough into a ball. On lightly floured surface, roll out dough ½ inch thick. Using a 2-inch biscuit cutter or sharp knife, cut dough into rounds. Transfer biscuits to prepared baking sheets. Bake 20 to 25 minutes, or until well browned. Turn off the heat and allow biscuits to dry in oven for several hours. Store in refrigerator, or place in freezer bags and freeze. *Makes about 36 biscuits.*

MacDigger's Highland Graham Biscuits

2 cups graham cracker crumbs
1 cup unbleached all-purpose flour
1 tablespoon baking powder
½ teaspoon salt
½ cup corn oil
1 cup milk

Preheat oven to 425° F. and oil 2 or 3 baking sheets.

In a mixing bowl, combine cracker crumbs, flour, baking powder, and salt. In a small bowl or measuring cup, mix oil and milk, then stir into flour mixture.

Turn dough out on lightly floured surface and knead lightly, until soft and well mixed. Roll out dough ½ inch thick and cut into 1½-inch rounds. Place biscuits on prepared baking sheets about 1 inch apart. Bake 10 minutes, until lightly browned. Store cooled biscuits, covered, in refrigerator or freezer. *Makes about 42 biscuits.*

Signs of a Healthy Puppy
- bright eyes, with no discharge
- clean-smelling skin and ears
- even, well-aligned teeth
- good proportions for breed
- solid, without being heavy

Safety Tips for Puppies
- fence in area where puppy plays
- use safety gate in house to keep puppy in its own area
- block access to areas where puppy might hurt itself: stairs, pools, steep drops
- hide electrical cords
- remove breakable objects from precarious places
- remove traps, poisons, or insect or animal bait from puppy's outdoor play area

JEZEBEL'S PEANUT BUTTER BISCUITS

These snacks are full of energy for your dog. Be sure to use fresh 100 percent peanut butter without salt, sugar, or hydrogenated oils.

Burying bones is instinctive behavior. Early wild ancestors of the dog once stored food underground for use in leaner times.

It's possible that dogs learned to bark by imitating the sounds made by man. In the wild, wolves and wild dogs don't bark, they howl.

1½ cups whole wheat flour
½ cup soy flour
1 tablespoon baking powder
½ teaspoon salt
1 cup peanut butter, either creamy or chunky
¾ cup milk

Preheat oven to 400° F. and grease 2 baking sheets.

In a mixing bowl, combine whole wheat and soy flours, baking powder, and salt. In a blender, blend peanut butter and milk. Pour peanut butter mixture into dry ingredients and mix well. The dough should be soft.

Turn dough out on lightly floured surface and knead lightly. Roll out dough ¼ inch thick and cut into 2-inch squares. Place biscuits on baking sheets about 1 inch apart. Bake 15 minutes, or until lightly browned. Stored cooled biscuits, well wrapped, in refrigerator or freezer. *Makes about 18 biscuits.*

LOCH NESS SCONES

2 cups unbleached all-purpose flour
2 teaspoons baking powder
1 tablespoon sugar
½ teaspoon salt
¼ cup cold vegetable shortening
1 egg, lightly beaten
½ cup milk

Preheat oven to 400° F. and grease a baking sheet.

In a mixing bowl, combine flour, baking powder, sugar, and salt. Cut in shortening with a fork. In a small bowl, mix egg and milk, then lightly stir into flour mixture.

Turn dough out on lightly floured surface and knead gently for 1 or 2 turns. Roll out dough ½ inch thick and cut into 2-inch squares. Place scones on prepared baking sheet about 1 inch apart. Bake 15 minutes. *Makes about 18 scones.*

Canine Encounters

A chance meeting with a stray or territorial dog can be frightening because the dog's behavior can't be predicted. Here are some guidelines:

- speak calmly
- do not engage the dog in a stare-down because the dog will correctly interpret such behavior as a challenge
- maintain an upright posture; do not put your face and neck near the dog's mouth
- do not make any sudden moves
- if you are in an enclosed space, invite the dog to leave with you so that it gets the message that you're the boss
- do not block the dog's exit or prevent it from retreating

Love Snaps

Love me, love my dog.
—John Heywood,
   Proverbes, 1546

These crunchy liver biscuits will melt the heart of even the most aloof dog.

Training tip

Reward your dog with lots of praise and love rather than food. Love Snaps are a delicious treat that you can give your dog at any time but lesson time. It's a treat that exists for no other reason than to show your dog you love him.

2 cups unbleached all-purpose flour
1 cup cornmeal
1 teaspoon salt
1 large egg, lightly beaten
3 tablespoons vegetable oil
½ cup Chicken Stock (page 84)
2 teaspoons chopped parsley
1 cup chopped cooked chicken livers

Preheat oven to 400° F. and oil a large baking sheet.

Combine flour, cornmeal, and salt. In a small bowl, beat egg with oil, then add stock and parsley; mix well. Put one-third flour mixture in a mixing bowl and stir in one-third stock mixture. Continue adding dry and wet ingredients by thirds, stirring until all ingredients are well mixed. Fold in chicken livers, mixing well. Dough will be firm.

Turn dough out on lightly floured surface and knead briefly. Roll out dough ½ inch thick and cut out biscuits with small, heart-shaped cookie cutter. Place biscuits on prepared baking sheet about 1 inch apart. Bake 15 minutes, or until firm. Store in refrigerator. *Makes about 24 biscuits.*

HEALTH MUFFINS

1½ cups whole wheat flour
1 cup rolled oats
1 cup oat bran
2 teaspoons baking soda
1 teaspoon cinnamon
2 apples
½ cup raisins
1 egg, lightly beaten
¼ cup honey
3 tablespoons corn oil
1 cup milk

Preheat oven to 425° F. Line 24 muffin tins with paper forms.

In a mixing bowl, combine flour, oats, oat bran, baking soda, and cinnamon. Grate apples (with skins) into a bowl, then stir in raisins, egg, honey, and oil. Stir milk into flour mixture, blending well. Add apple mixture and mix well.

Spoon batter into muffin tins and bake 20 to 25 minutes, or until a toothpick inserted in center of a muffin comes out dry. These muffins freeze well. *Makes 24 muffins.*

You can create many variations of this basic high-fiber recipe by substituting, for the apples, grated pears, zucchini, or carrots. For the raisins, you may substitute chopped walnuts, pecans or currants. All are delicious and healthy for your dog.

SOY POWER DOG MUFFINS

Soy flour is very high in fiber and also contains 40 percent protein.

Like a bumper sticker, your dog makes a statement about who you are and your attitudes toward life. There are status dogs and dogs that have plummeted from popularity. In the twenties, fashionable women selected borzois to match their fur coats. In the fifties, Rin Tin Tin and Lassie were every kid's dream dogs. Recent favorites include the akita, bouvier, and Shar-Pei.

1 egg, lightly beaten
1 cup milk
¼ cup corn oil
1½ teaspoons baking powder
½ teaspoon baking soda
½ teaspoon salt
1 cup whole wheat flour
½ cup soy flour
½ cup bran flakes (miller's bran)
½ cup raisins

Preheat oven to 400° F. Line 12 muffin tins with paper forms.

In a mixing bowl, combine egg, milk, and oil. Stir in baking powder, baking soda, and salt. Combine whole wheat and soy flours and bran, then add slowly to egg mixture, beating until the batter is well mixed. Fold in raisins.

Spoon batter into muffin tins. Bake 10 minutes. *Makes 12 muffins.*

FEATHERWEIGHT RICE CAKES

1 cup cooked rice
1 cup milk
2 tablespoons corn oil
1 cup unbleached all-purpose flour
1 tablespoon baking powder
½ teaspoon salt
3 egg whites.

Preheat oven to 400° F. Line 18 muffin tins with paper forms.

In a mixing bowl, combine rice, milk and oil. Combine flour, baking powder, and salt, then stir into rice mixture. In another bowl, beat egg whites until stiff. Stir one-third of whites into batter, then fold in remaining whites. Mixture will be very thin.

Spoon batter into muffin tins. Bake 25 to 30 minutes, or until light and puffy. *Makes 18 muffins.*

These light, airy puffs are perfect for a dog on a bland, simple diet.

Sometimes people select a pet for qualities they lack themselves but nevertheless wish to project as their own. A person who lacks self-confidence may select a German shepherd or a doberman pinscher because these dogs stand for courage and aggressiveness. The illegal "sport" of dog fighting with pit bulls no doubt enables their owners to act out their aggression via their animals.

GINGERBREAD MAILMEN

The mailman is someone with whom most dogs develop some kind of relationship—for better or worse. Our fortunate mailman is greeted daily with slurpy dog kisses that leave prints all over the entry door's glass panes. These crunchy cookies will help clean your pet's teeth.

½ cup molasses
2 tablespoons honey
½ cup water
¼ cup vegetable oil
3 cups unbleached all-purpose flour
1 teaspoon baking soda
½ teaspoon cinnamon
½ teaspoon ground cloves
2 tablespoons ground fresh ginger
½ teaspoon salt
¼ cup raisins

In a medium mixing bowl, combine molasses, honey, water, and oil. In another bowl, mix together flour, baking soda, cinnamon, cloves, ginger, and salt. Stir flour mixture slowly into molasses mixture, mixing well with a wooden spoon. Divide dough in half, shape each piece into a ball, wrap in plastic wrap, and refrigerate for several hours.

Preheat oven to 350° F. and oil a baking sheet.

On a lightly floured surface, roll out dough ¼ inch thick. Cut into gingerbread men with cookie cutter or into free-form shapes and transfer to baking sheet. Press in raisins for eyes and buttons. Bake 10 to 15 minutes, or until firm and lightly browned around the edges. *Makes 12 cookies.*

CHEESE DREAMS

½ cup grated Cheddar cheese
½ cup cottage cheese
2 tablespoons vegetable oil
1 teaspoon salt
½ teaspoon Worcestershire sauce
2 cups unbleached all-purpose flour
¾ cup finely chopped walnuts

Preheat oven to 400° F.

In a large bowl, mix together cheddar and cottage cheese. Add oil, salt, and Worcestershire sauce. Slowly stir in flour, mixing well until dough can be easily molded.

Break off marble-size pieces of dough, shape into balls, and roll in walnuts. Place on ungreased baking sheet and bake 20 minutes, or until golden brown. Store cooled cookies in tightly covered container in refrigerator. *Makes about 48 cookies.*

Cheese is universally loved by dogs, who won't turn down even the most odoriferous morsel. A little grated cheese will usually tempt the pickiest dog to approach the bowl and consider the rest of the meal. Because it is so concentrated, cheese should be fed sparingly to dieting dogs.

BLUE RIBBON BLINTZES

To make a dog into a top-notch champion requires a considerable amount of time and money. It's not unusual for a best-in-show winner to cost his owners over $20,000 for a year's worth of travel, handling, and fees. Show dogs are under a lot of stress, and their diets must be supplemented. Aside from tolerating many longs hours traveling and waiting in a crate, show dogs are also slaves to the grooming routine.

Dogs are gaga about these blintzes. Because the filling is so rich, reserve for special occasions.

Filling
1 cup cottage or ricotta cheese
1 egg
1 tablespoon unbleached all-purpose flour
Pinch of salt

Crêpes
¾ cup unbleached all-purpose flour
2 eggs
1 cup milk
2 tablespoons unsalted butter, melted, plus butter for frying blintzes
½ teaspoon salt

To make filling, place cheese, egg, flour, and salt in mixing bowl and beat until well blended. Reserve.

To make crêpes, place flour, eggs, milk, butter, and salt in a blender or food processor container and process until batter is smooth. Pour batter into 1-quart measuring cup.

Heat a 7½- to 8-inch skillet or omelet pan over medium heat and brush lightly with butter. Pour in one-eighth of batter and tilt pan quickly so batter covers entire bottom. Cook until edges of crêpes begin to curl up. The bottom should be golden brown and the top should be covered with fine bubbles. Place the crêpe, cooked side down, on a clean towel. Continue making crêpes until batter is used up. Crêpes may be layered between sheets of wax paper until you are ready to fill them.

To fill, turn crêpes cooked sides up. Put a heaping tablespoon of filling on lower third of each pancake and roll up. Heat 2 tablespoons butter in a heavy skillet over moderate heat, add blintzes, and brown on all sides. Serve at once. *Makes 8 blintzes.*

HUSH PUPPY CORN PONE

2 cups cornmeal
3 tablespoons corn oil
½ teaspoon salt
1 cup water

Preheat oven to 375° F. and grease a baking sheet.

Place cornmeal, oil, and salt in a bowl. In a saucepan, bring water to a boil over high heat and pour over cornmeal mixture, stirring well. Allow mixture to cool 10 minutes. Form mush into 2-inch patties with your hands. (It helps to moisten your hands with oil or water.)

Place pones on prepared baking sheet. Bake 30 minutes, or until firm. *Makes about 18 biscuits.*

Hush puppies are deep-fried biscuits. The name originated around Southern campfires, when biscuits would be tossed to the dogs to keep them quiet. This recipe isn't deep-fried and heavy the way true Southern hush puppies are, but your dog will love these light, easily prepared patties.

CORN CRISPS

Corn is a nutritious staple not only for dogs but for much of the world's population. Dogs love fresh corn, and they take particular pleasure in gnawing on the cob, where the germ contains most of the vitamins.

. . . a dog is really a subservient creature by nature, longing to trust his true love to someone's heart.
—Barbara Woodhouse,
   No Bad Dogs

2 cups cornmeal
½ teaspoon baking soda
½ teaspoon salt
1 cup buttermilk
3 tablespoons corn oil
2 tablespoons honey
Butter

Place cornmeal, baking soda, salt, buttermilk, oil, and honey in a blender or food processor container and process until batter is smooth. Melt butter in a skillet; ladle 2 tablespoons of batter into skillet for each 3-inch round. Cook until golden brown on both sides, about 5 minutes in all. *Makes about 24 pancakes.*

OATCAKES

2 cups milk
1 cup rolled oats
1 cup unbleached all-purpose flour
1½ teaspoons baking powder
½ teaspoon baking soda
1 teaspoon cinnamon
½ teaspoon ground ginger
1 teaspoon salt
1 egg, beaten
3 tablespoons unsalted butter

In a large saucepan, heat milk over moderately low heat until just warmed through. Stir in oats and allow to stand 10 minutes.

Combine flour, baking powder, baking soda, cinnamon, ginger, and salt. Add egg to oatmeal mixture, then stir in flour mixture. Add oil. Batter will be very thick.

In a large, heavy skillet over medium heat, melt the butter. Spoon in 2 tablespoons of batter for each oatcake and cook until golden brown on both sides. Serve hot; they taste delicious with a touch of maple syrup, which dogs adore. Refrigerate remaining oatcakes. *Makes about 36 pancakes.*

Like cornmeal, oatmeal should be a staple grain in your dog's diet. Oats have a soothing effect, and they are useful in helping to cleanse the system and assist in tissue growth, a valuable aid for the sick or convalescing dog. Oats in any form make a delicious canine breakfast or midday snack. These oatcakes are inexpensive, simple to prepare, and nourishing.

How to Brush Your Dog's Teeth

What to use:
- baking soda and water
- hydrogen peroxide
- dog toothpaste

Apply with:
- cheesecloth
- cotton swab
- foam applicator

Some dogs have tartar-free teeth for a lifetime. It seems to depend on diet and genetic endowment. If your dog accumulates tartar, increase the crunchy foods in the diet and brush as necessary. Some dogs will need a brushing once a month, others weekly. A special dog toothpaste, C.E.T., available from veterinarians, contains a peroxide solution that helps to dissolve tartar buildup. You can also obtain special dog toothbrushes from your vet.

Since most dogs aren't too enthusiastic about having their teeth brushed, it's helpful to do a small area, or even just a single tooth at a time. It's better to teach your dog to tolerate the cleaning of a few teeth than to get into a power struggle and have the dog decide he will never let you near his mouth again. If you're gentle and introduce the regime slowly, he may even get to like the special attention.

DOG BREAKFASTS

The average dog has a busy daily agenda that requires a nourishing breakfast. While it needn't be a full meal, your dog will appreciate the bit of extra energy that a little light food provides. If you remember how dragged out you feel if you miss a meal or two during the day, imagine how difficult it must be for dogs to fast until dinner, day after day. Also, one heavy meal at day's end can increase your pet's weight, especially if your dog has little else to do after the evening meal but sleep and convert those unused calories to dog blubber.

A light breakfast will set your dog up for the day. It's easy to prepare a very simple meal, since most dogs like cereal—shredded wheat, cream of wheat or rice, wheat germ, oatmeal, or bran. The cereal can be mixed with plain yogurt, milk, or stock. Don't rule out conventional warm breakfast foods that people eat. Most dogs love pancakes and French toast. You can incorporate leftovers in a creative way: vegetables, beans, cheeses—all are a pleasing breakfast for your dog.

MASHED POTATO BALLS

4 cups mashed potatoes
1 tablespoon chopped Italian parsley
Salt
Freshly ground black pepper
2 egg yolks
2 tablespoons unsalted butter
1 teaspoon paprika

Preheat oven to 400° F. and grease a large baking dish.

Place potatoes, parsley, and salt and pepper to taste in a mixing bowl; stir until combined. Add egg yolks and mix well. Shape into balls the size of walnuts and place in baking dish. Dot tops with butter, sprinkle lightly with paprika, and bake about 10 minutes, or until browned. *Makes about 40 potato balls.*

Generations of working sheep-dogs have been sustained on a potato diet, yet many people mistakenly believe that potatoes are harmful to dogs. Canines particularly love baked potato skins, which are an excellent snack. When preparing potatoes, be sure to cut out any budding sprouts or green areas which may contain toxic material.

RICE PORRIDGE

This porridge has an Oriental flavor and is perfect for cold mornings. You can prepare a large batch to parcel out during the week—just reheat the rice in a double boiler. To tempt finicky eaters, pour a little Chicken Stock (page 84) or Basic Dog Broth (page 83) over the porridge. The rice base makes this dish easily tolerated by dogs with digestive problems.

2 cups uncooked rice
3 quarts water
2 tablespoons vegetable oil
2 cups 1-inch pieces of bok choy or Swiss chard
2 scallions, finely chopped
1 cup chopped cooked meat or poultry
1 teaspoon grated fresh ginger
1 tablespoon tamari sauce
1 tablespoon sesame seed oil

In a large saucepan or Dutch oven, bring rice and water to a boil over medium heat. Reduce heat and simmer rice, covered, 30 minutes.

In a large skillet, heat vegetable oil; add bok choy or chard and scallions and stir-fry 2 minutes. Transfer stir-fried vegetables to pan with rice. Add chopped meat, ginger, tamari, and sesame seed oil; return rice mixture to a boil over high heat, stirring. Reduce heat and cook mixture 30 minutes more. *Makes 4½ quarts.*

PRAIRIE COOKOUT RICE AND BEANS

1 cup uncooked brown rice
2½ cups water
2 tablespoons vegetable oil
1 carrot, chopped
1 zucchini, sliced
1 scallion, chopped
1 cup Chicken Stock (page 84)
1 can (15½ ounces) pink or kidney beans, drained
1 tablespoon tamari sauce

In a small saucepan, bring rice and water to a boil over high heat. Reduce heat and simmer rice, covered, 45 minutes, or until tender.

In a skillet, heat oil over medium heat; add carrot and zucchini and stir-fry 2 to 3 minutes. Stir in scallion and cook 1 minute longer. Add beans, stock, and tamari to skillet and combine mixture well.

Place rice in dog bowl and spoon bean mixture over it. Refrigerate leftovers, well covered; reheat beans and rice together. *Makes 3 cups rice and 1 quart beans.*

This is a perfect meal in itself, a good balance of protein and complex carbohydrates, and so simple to prepare that you can easily cook it over a campfire.

How to Pick up a Dog
Whatever the size, a dog needs to feel secure when it's picked up and can't rely on its own four feet for support. The method is the same for small and large dogs alike, although it's less daunting with a lightweight pup.

Grasp the dog in two places: under the lower chest, but in front of the forelegs, and in back of the hind legs.

FRENCH TOAST

Fortunately, dogs aren't picky about day-old bread, so this is an excellent way to avoid wasting food. Any combination of breads will do.

Cats usually resent the intrusion of a new puppy into the household. The balance of power has been temporarily disturbed, and as the cat finds itself overpowered by a boisterous puppy who isn't yet old enough to show any respect, the cat may move out of the house for a while. As a safety precaution, trim the cat's claws to prevent slashing and damage to the pup's eyes.

3 to 4 tablespoons unsalted butter
½ loaf day-old bread, cut into 1-inch cubes
4 large eggs
¾ cup milk
½ teaspoon cinnamon

In a large, heavy skillet, melt butter over medium heat. Add bread and cook, tossing bread cubes occasionally so that they brown lightly and evenly. In a small bowl, beat eggs with milk and cinnamon. Pour egg mixture over bread and fry until bread is well browned. *Makes about 1 quart French toast.*

Variation:
For delicious cheese French toast, omit the cinnamon and add ½ cup grated cheese—Cheddar, Gruyère, Muenster—to egg mixture.

CHICKEN SCRAPPLE

2 cups cornmeal
1 cup oatmeal
3 cups Chicken Stock (page 84)
2 cups cooked chicken, cut into small pieces
¼ cup finely chopped onion
1 tablespoon ground thyme
Salt
Freshly ground black pepper
Butter or vegetable oil for frying

In the top of a double boiler, combine cornmeal, oatmeal, and stock; cook grains over boiling water 30 minutes. Add chicken, onion, thyme, and salt and pepper to taste; stir well. The mixture will be very thick. Grease a 9-inch loaf pan and pour in cornmeal mixture. Smooth top with a rubber spatula, cover with plastic wrap, and refrigerate overnight.

Cut scrapple into slices. Heat butter or oil in skillet over moderate heat, add scrapple, and fry until golden on both sides. *Makes one 1 large loaf.*

This is a variation on the famous Pennsylvania Dutch scrapple that is usually made from pork and organ meats. The chicken is a readily available ingredient, and the oatmeal is a new addition.

BAKED DOG GRRRITS

Most dogs are not interested in hominy grits served plain, so it's advisable to embellish them with a delicious gravy or with cheese.

1 cup hominy grits
5 cups water
2 large eggs, beaten
1½ cups shredded Cheddar cheese
1 cup milk
1 tablespoon Worcestershire sauce
Salt
Freshly ground black pepper
1 tablespoon unsalted butter

In a medium saucepan, bring grits and water to a boil over high heat. Reduce heat and cook grits, stirring frequently, for 20 minutes, or until very thick.

Preheat oven to 350° F. and butter a shallow 3-quart baking dish.

Transfer grits to a mixing bowl and beat in eggs, ¾ cup of cheese, milk, and Worcestershire sauce. Pour mixture into baking dish and spread remaining cheese on top. Sprinkle with salt and pepper to taste, dot with butter, and bake 1 hour. Allow grits to stand 5 to 10 minutes before serving. Wrap leftovers well in plastic wrap or foil and refrigerate or freeze. *Makes 2 quarts grits.*

OMELETS AND OTHER EGG DISHES

That island of England breeds very valiant creatures: their mastiffs are of unmatchable courage.
—William Shakespeare
  King Richard II, Act III

Dogs love eggs fixed almost any way. Eggs provide easily digestible, high-quality protein (there are about 78 grams of protein in a dozen eggs) and are extremely versatile and convenient. There's probably not one dog owner who hasn't added an egg to a dog's food at one time or another. For toy dogs, a single egg is just the right amount of food. Because dogs are not prone to cholesterol buildup, they can safely eat more eggs than their masters.

POACHER'S PARADISE

6 *strips bacon*
2 *cups half-and-half*
3 *large eggs*
3 *slices dark bread, cut into bite-size pieces*
3 *teaspoons freshly grated Parmesan cheese*

In a skillet, fry bacon over medium heat until crisp. Drain bacon on paper towels and crumble. Reserve.

In a saucepan, heat half-and-half over medium heat until it simmers. Break eggs separately into pan and poach until whites are cooked. Place bread in deep bowl, lift eggs out of saucepan and place on bread. Sprinkle with cheese and bacon. Pour poaching liquid over eggs and serve at once. *Makes 3 poached eggs with toast, or approximately three 2-cup servings.*

Variation:
For dieting dogs, substitute Basic Dog Broth (page 83) or Chicken Stock (page 84) for half-and-half.

Our Dogs, an English journal published in 1735, described the roving gangs of stray dogs whose unruly behavior and passion for fresh eggs posed a serious problem at the time. These dogs "infested the roads in great numbers, barking and snapping at the horse's heels and causing many a rider to fall; . . . they poached the game, sucked the pheasants' eggs and resorted to all manner of shenanigans for which they should be taxed as a means of control." The following recipe will surely keep the most resolute wanderer at home—at least through breakfast—and the Parmesan cheese and bacon will tempt the older dog who is picky about its food.

FOO DOG YUNG

The favorite of the Imperial family in Peking, the Pekingese is the model for the numerous Foo Dog statues that are carved in ivory or cast in bronze. The Pekingese can be traced to the Tang Dynasty of the eighth century, and it's said that the purest strains were the exclusive property of the Imperial family. Considered to be sacred, these tiny "sleeve dogs" were cared for and carefully bred by palace eunuchs.

Good meat fillings for this Oriental specialty are liver, chicken, beef and pork.

3 large eggs, beaten
1½ teaspoons soy sauce
1½ teaspoons cornstarch
½ cup Chicken Stock (page 84)
1 tablespoon oil, or as needed
3 tablespoons finely chopped onion
3 to 6 tablespoons chopped celery
½ cup cooked ground meat or cooked flaked fish

In a small bowl, beat egg with soy sauce. Blend cornstarch into stock. Heat oil in small skillet over medium-low heat. Add onion and celery and stir-fry until onion is translucent. Add more oil, if necessary; add meat or fish and stir-fry 2 minutes. Transfer mixture to a bowl.

Add a little more oil, if needed, to skillet; add egg and cook, stirring gently, until egg is half-cooked. Add meat mixture and stock; continue to cook, stirring vigorously, until eggs are fully cooked and liquid is absorbed. *Makes about 1½ cups eggs and meat.*

EGGS AND TRUFFLE

4 large eggs
2 tablespoons unsalted butter
½ cup milk
¼ cup dry white wine
Salt
Freshly ground white pepper
1 white or black truffle (or substitute a large mushroom)

In a bowl, beat eggs with a whisk until well mixed. In a small skillet, heat butter over medium heat until brown. Reduce heat, add eggs, and cook, stirring often with a fork or spatula. As soon as eggs are set, pour in milk and blend well. Add salt and pepper to taste. Transfer mixture to 2 or 3 dog bowls and grate truffle over top of eggs. *Makes 1 generous cup eggs.*

AFTER A LIGHT LUNCH of EGGS AND TRUFFLE, CHAUNCEY PEDIGREE IV ATTENDS A CHARITY POLO MATCH AT HIS CLUB.

Truffle dogs were once used to scent out this rare and expensive delicacy that grows near the roots of the oak tree. The truffle dog is thought to be descended from poodle stock. Dark and quiet and equipped with an extraordinarily keen nose, the truffle dogs dug for the prized fungus, then lifted it to the surface with their forefeet. It was to their masters' advantage that the dogs were quiet, for the best truffles were located on large estates, and more often than not the truffle dog's master was a poacher. The reward for the truffle dog was a share of its master's bread and cheese, but not the truffle itself. In this recipe, that inequity is redressed. Clearly meant for a once-in-a-lifetime treat, this dish will make some dog swoon with happiness.

CANINE QUICHE

This recipe is especially good for finicky toys and under-weight dogs. You can vary the taste by adding a number of delicious fillings; cheese or chopped cooked liver, kidney, tripe, ham, sausage, or bacon.

3 or 4 large eggs
¾ cup heavy cream
¾ cup milk
5 tablespoons chopped cooked meat or grated cheese
Salt
Freshly ground black pepper
9-inch pie shell, baked and cooled

Preheat oven to 375° F.

In a mixing bowl, whisk together eggs, cream, and milk. Stir in meat or cheese and salt and pepper to taste. Pour mixture into pie shell and bake until puffy and light brown on top, about 35 to 40 minutes.

Allow quiche to cool slightly before serving. *Makes one 9-inch pie.*

EGG SALAD

5 hard-cooked eggs
1 small Bermuda onion, finely chopped
¼ cup chopped fresh dill or parsley or 1 teaspoon curry powder
½ cup mayonnaise
¼ cup Dijon mustard
Salt
Freshly ground black pepper
2 or 3 slices bread, preferably pumpernickel or rye, cut into bite-size pieces

Peel eggs, cut into small wedges, and place in mixing bowl. In another bowl, combine onion, mayonnaise, mustard, herb or curry powder, and salt and pepper to taste. Pour sauce over eggs and toss lightly. Spread bread pieces on plate and distribute egg mixture over them.

Leftover egg salad should be covered tightly and refrigerated for no longer than 1 day. *Makes 2 cups egg salad.*

This recipe contains raw onion, a vegetable that some dogs find objectionable. You may need to experiment to see what works best for your dog. In addition to their beneficial toning and cleansing effects, onions are thought to be useful in discouraging worms and other parasites.

I'M NOT UPSET, MON CHERE—REALLY—IT'S THE ONIONS!!

BASIC OMELET FOR DOGS

3 large eggs
Salt
Freshly ground black pepper
3 tablespoons unsalted butter
2 tablespoons chopped cooked meat, poultry, or fish or grated cheese

In a mixing bowl, beat eggs vigorously with whisk or fork for 30 seconds. Stir in salt and pepper to taste.

Melt butter in omelet pan and over medium heat. When butter is brown and releases a nutty aroma, pour eggs into pan. Stir eggs for a few seconds then cook, sliding pan back and forth over heat to keep eggs from sticking. As omelet begins to set, slide spatula under edge, allowing creamy, uncooked liquid to flow into center of pan. Omelet is cooked when eggs are creamy on top, but no longer runny.

Spoon meat over omelet, tilt pan, and fold omelet in half over filling. Slide omelet onto plate and serve immediately. *Makes 1 large omelet.*

Fear of Flying

Because of recent improvements to insure the health and comfort of dog passengers, cargo section temperature is now better regulated in flight, with a range of 45 to 85° F., and dogs no longer arrive at destinations frozen, asphyxiated, bruised, or battered.

But although conditions are safer, air travel is still unpleasant for dogs, who are subject to the roar of the engines, pressure changes, and possible breathing problems. Short-nosed breeds must have floor-to-ceiling ventilation and should fly only it it's absolutely necessary.

Dogs in transit should *never* be given human tranquilizers, nor should they be muzzled.

SONORA BREAKFAST

8 ounces chorizo sausage, casings removed
2 tablespoons unsalted butter
¼ cup finely chopped onion
3 large eggs
Salt
Freshly ground black pepper
½ cup grated sharp Cheddar cheese
Steamed rice (optional)

In a heavy skillet, cook chorizo over medium heat, breaking up sausage with a wooden spoon. When sausage is brown, remove from pan with slotted spoon and drain on paper towels.

Pour out any fat remaining in skillet, add 1 tablespoon butter, and melt over medium heat. Add onion and sauté until translucent.

In mixing bowl, beat eggs with fork or whisk for 30 seconds. Add salt and pepper to taste, then stir in cheese. Add remaining butter to skillet with onions; when melted, return sausage to skillet and heat 1 minute. Pour in egg mixture and cook over medium heat, lifting cooked portion of omelet until eggs are no longer runny. Fold in half and serve with steamed rice as an accompaniment. *Makes 1 large omelet.*

Calm Down

This recipe will feed a gaggle of chihuahuas, curious little dogs who prefer each other's company to that of other dogs. By the time the Spanish invaded Mexico in the sixteenth century, chihuahuas filled a number of roles in Aztec society. Revered by wealthy Aztecs, who believed blue-colored versions to be sacred guides who led the souls of the dead through the underworld, the dogs were the object of religious sacrifice. At the other end of the spectrum, the peasants, who valued the appeasement of hunger more than canine spiritual guidance, often made a meal of these tiny animals.

The spice of chorizo and the tang of Cheddar cheese will help to warm the blood of this delicate dog on a cold day.

TAIL-WAGGER'S EGGS WITH SAFFRON RICE

A sure sign of dog delight is the excited wag of his tail, especially in anticipation of dinner. A dog's tail is one of his most expressive nonverbal communicators and is used to indicate fear and aggression as well as joy.

1 cup uncooked rice
2 cups Chicken Stock (page 84) or 1 cup water and 1 cup stock
Pinch of saffron threads
1 tablespoon vinegar
2 to 4 large eggs
¼ cup Canine Curry Sauce (page 161)

In a saucepan, bring rice and stock to a boil. Add saffron, cover pan, reduce heat to very low, and simmer rice 18 to 20 minutes, or until tender.

In another saucepan or a skillet, bring to a simmer enough water to cover eggs, then add vinegar. One at a time, break eggs into a saucer and slide into simmering liquid. Poach eggs 5 minutes. Meanwhile, spoon cooked rice onto plate. Remove eggs from liquid with slotted spoon and arrange over rice. Pour curry sauce on top and serve. *Makes about 3 cups eggs and rice.*

EGG AND GIZZARD PUDDING

1 cup chicken gizzards
1 quart milk
2 large raw eggs
1 tablespoon Dijon mustard
Salt
Freshly ground black pepper
6 slices white bread
4 hard-cooked eggs, sliced
2 cups beef stock

Preheat oven to 350° F. Grease a 13 × 9-inch baking dish.

Place gizzards in saucepan with water to cover by 1 inch. Bring to a boil, then reduce heat and simmer gizzards, covered, 1 hour. Drain, cool, and cut gizzards into small pieces.

In a mixing bowl, beat together milk, raw eggs, mustard, and salt and pepper to taste. Arrange bread on bottom of baking dish; pour egg mixture over bread. Arrange hard-cooked eggs and gizzards over bread and pour stock on top. Cover baking dish with lid or foil and bake 45 minutes. Cool pie slightly, but serve while still warm. *Makes 2½ quarts pudding.*

This bread pudding requires very little assembly time and is made with the simplest of ingredients. Gizzards are an exceptional source of protein, containing 91 grams of that nutrient. If you've been throwing out the gizzards that come packed with whole chickens, this recipe will give you a perfect excuse to wrap them well and freeze.

While you're waiting for this pie to bake, take your dog outside for a game of Frisbee. In 1978, canine champ Martha Faye and her master Dave Johnson set a remarkable record of 334.6 feet for canine distance in Frisbee throw-and-catch.

LAZYBONES EGG PUDDING

It's the paprika in the pudding that gives this special dish its zing. Not only that, it's also a cinch to make—just the ticket to perk up the taste buds of the dog who's bored with everyday fare.

1 raw egg
1 cup milk
½ cup Chicken Stock (page 84)
Salt
Freshly ground black pepper
2 hard-cooked eggs, chopped
6 slices bread, torn into strips
1 cup coarsely chopped cooked chicken
2 tablespoons unsalted butter
Pinch of paprika

Preheat oven to 350° F. and grease a 3-quart baking dish.

In mixing bowl, combine raw egg, milk, stock, and salt and pepper to taste; beat well. Stir in chopped eggs. Arrange bread and chicken in baking dish. Pour egg and milk mixture over all, dot top with butter, and sprinkle lightly with paprika. Bake about 30 minutes, or until all the liquid is absorbed and pudding is lightly browned around edges. Cool slightly before serving. *Makes 1½ quarts pudding.*

Kibble, like dog biscuits, is an outgrowth of the "dog cakes" of the nineteenth century, essentially a version of the hardtack that sustained early seagoing travelers, human and canine alike. While there are many dry commercial foods on the market, most rely primarily upon a combination of wheat, corn, or rice; meat or poultry by-product or "meal"; and lesser amounts of dairy products, fat, preservatives, and supplements.

Protein content varies considerably in these products, from 20 to 30 percent, depending upon brand and your dog's needs. The protein available to your dog, however, depends upon the quality of ingredients and the relative digestibility of the protein in the food. For example, wheat gluten protein is only half as digestible as milk or beef.

While most reputable brands supplement their foods with vitamins and minerals, it is important to realize that many nutrients are lost during processing and storage. For this reason, it's not advisable to buy dog food in large quantities, even though it may be more economical or convenient to do so. One dog food retailer I spoke with told me that he believes the food is already several months old by the time it reaches his shelves, and for this reason encourages all of his customers to supplement their pets' diets with high-quality vitamins and minerals.

Clearly then, to insure freshness, it's best to buy kibble in small quantities or to make your own, which you should feed to your dog as soon as practical, tightly sealing and refrigerating or freezing the unused portions. Ingredients such as bonemeal, brewer's yeast, and rye flour are readily available at health food stores.

MULTI-GRAIN DOG KIBBLE

2 cups whole wheat flour
1½ cups all-purpose unbleached flour
½ cup soy flour
1 cup cornmeal
1 cup nonfat dry milk powder
1 cup rolled oats
½ cup wheat germ
½ cup brewer's yeast
1 tablespoon salt
1 large egg
5 tablespoons corn oil
3 cups water

Preheat oven to 350° F. and grease two 13 × 9-inch baking sheets.

In a large mixing bowl, combine whole wheat, all-purpose and soy flours, cornmeal, milk powder, oats, brewer's yeast, and salt. In a small bowl, combine egg and corn oil. Stir water into dry ingredients, then add egg mixture, mixing well. The batter will be thin.

Divide batter between baking sheets, spreading evenly ½ inch thick, as though for pizza. Bake 45 minutes. Cool kibble, then break into small pieces. Store in covered container in refrigerator, or divide into individual servings, place in freezer bags, and freeze. *Makes 20 cups kibble.*

Your dog will love eating this basic kibble as often as you choose to serve it. It's especially good as the base for a stew or a delicious gravy.

Variation:
For delicious doggie pizza, sprinkle crumbled cooked sausage, bacon, dried fish, ham, or salami on top before baking.

Don't roughhouse or tease a growing pup or encourage him to grab your hands, arms, or feet with his mouth. What seems cute in a two-month-old pup can become dangerous to life and limb once the adorable creature grows permanent teeth. Remember that a dog's jaw is eight times more powerful than a human's.

CORN KIBBLE

Cornmeal makes this even crunchier than Multi-Grain Kibble.

Dogs tend to respect their owners more if they're taught basic obedience skills. They love to learn and actually need tasks in order to put their intelligence to use and to gratify their innate wish to please.

2 cups whole wheat flour
2 cups cornmeal
1 cup nonfat dry milk powder
¼ cup brewer's yeast
1 tablespoon bonemeal
1 teaspoon salt
3 cups water
½ cup corn oil

Preheat oven to 350° F. and grease two 13 × 9-inch baking sheets.

In a large mixing bowl, combine whole wheat, cornmeal, milk powder, flour, brewer's yeast, bonemeal, and salt. Stir water into dry ingredients, then add corn oil, mixing well. The batter will be thin.

Divide batter between baking sheets, spreading evenly ½ inch thick, as though for pizza. Bake 45 minutes. Cool kibble, then break into small pieces. Store in covered container in refrigerator, or divide into individual servings, place in freezer bags, and freeze. *Makes 8 cups kibble.*

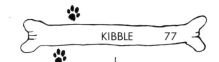

OAT AND RICE KIBBLE

2 cups all-purpose unbleached flour
1 cup rolled oats
1 cup cooked brown rice
½ cup nonfat dry milk powder
1 tablespoon bonemeal
1 egg
3 tablespoons corn oil
2 tablespoons tamari sauce
1 cup water

Preheat oven to 350° F. and grease one large baking sheet.

In a large mixing bowl, combine flour, oats, rice, milk powder, and bonemeal. In a small bowl, combine egg, corn oil, and tamari sauce. Stir water into dry ingredients, then add egg mixture, mixing well. The batter will be thin.

Spread batter evenly on baking sheet, ½ inch thick, as though for pizza. Bake 45 minutes. Cool kibble, then break into small pieces. Store in covered container in refrigerator, or divide into individual servings, place in freezer bags, and freeze. *Makes 6 cups kibble.*

The brown rice keeps this kibble soft and moist.

Deskunking a Dog

Give the dog a tomato juice bath, but take care to keep the juice out of your dog's eyes, and rinse the eyes well with water. A dog who has been "skunked" in the face can develop conjunctivitis. Because the odor is so strong, you can expect to administer the cure several times. You can also use products that are specially made to remove *eau de* skunk—Skunk Off is one to try. To help tame the odor inside the house, try boiling white vinegar. The fumes will distract you, if nothing else.

Cheesy Kasha Kibble

Cakelike and moist in texture, this kibble contains the grated cheese dogs finds irresistible.

Training a man takes time. Some men are a little slow to respond, but a dog who makes allowances and tries to put himself in the man's place will be rewarded with a loyal pal.
—Corey Ford, *Every Dog Should Own His Own Man*

2 cups whole wheat flour
½ cup soy flour
1 cup cooked kasha (buckwheat groats)
½ cup safflower oil
1½ cups water
1 tablespoon tamari sauce
1 cup coarsely grated Cheddar cheese

Preheat oven to 350° F. and grease a large baking sheet.

In a large mixing bowl, combine whole wheat and soy flours and kasha; mix well. In a small bowl, blend oil, water, and tamari. Stir liquid into dry ingredients, mixing well. Fold in grated cheese. Spread mixture ½ inch thick on baking sheet and bake 25 minutes. Cool kibble, then break into small pieces. *Makes 4 cups kibble.*

CARNIVOROUS KIBBLE

2 cups whole wheat flour
1 cup rye flour
1 cup nonfat dry milk powder
1 teaspoon bonemeal
½ teaspoon salt
2 eggs
½ cup corn oil
2 cloves garlic, minced
2 tablespoons Worcestershire sauce
1½ cups water
2 cups (about 1 pound) cooked ground beef, pork, or veal

Preheat oven to 350° F. and grease a large baking sheet.

In a large mixing bowl, combine whole wheat and rye flours, milk powder, bonemeal, and salt. In a small bowl, beat eggs, then blend in oil. Stir in garlic and Worcestershire sauce. Add water to flour mixture and blend well. Fold in egg mixture and mix thoroughly. Add meat and press it into dough, distributing evenly.

Spread mixture ½ inch thick on baking sheet and bake 45 minutes. Cool kibble, then break into bite-size chunks. Refrigerate and serve within 2 days, or freeze in individual portions. *Makes 4 cups kibble.*

This pizza for pooches is a good way to use up scraps of meat left over from roasts and stews. Be sure to keep this kibble refrigerated.

Extra! Extra!

Crime-Stopping Dog Passes Up Birthday Dinner

Dox, a German shepherd, helped to catch more than 400 criminals in his fifteen years of service with the police force in Turin, Italy. Along with his police master, Dox was a frequent and welcome diner in Turin's trattorias. On his birthday, the dog was allowed to select a free meal in any of his regular stops.

On his thirteenth birthday, Dox seemed undecided about where to go for his usual celebratory dinner of pasta and pork, and he pulled his master from restaurant to restaurant. Suddenly, with a great whiff, he entered a small restaurant and headed directly for a man eating in a dark corner of the room. Dox's master immediately recognized the man as a criminal who had eluded the team six years before. But Dox still remembered the man's scent after six years and had tracked him down.

—from *Seven True Dog Stories*, by Margaret Davidson

Many timid, high-strung dogs are prone to be suspicious and may bite or attack without much provocation. Experts say that small, nervous dogs are more likely to bite than larger ones. It must be difficult to be small and jittery in a world full of much larger, lumbering dogs.

According to Beatrice Lydecker, author of *What the Animals Tell Me*, "silent picture" communication works; you simply have to learn how to tune in to their tiny minds and receive their teeny transmissions. (P.S. I took my cat to her for a consultation, and the cat lied to her, something a dog would never do.)

Here's a helpful exercise for your skittish pet.

Bone Appétit! Visualization Exercise for Timid Dogs

- Sit in front of your dog.
- Visualize him in a stressful situation.
- Visualize him handling the situation with courage and confidence.
- See him complete the encounter successfully and walk off wagging his tail confidently.

SOUPS

Most dogs are enthusiastic soup lovers, preferring first to lap up the meaty broth and then to savor the rest of the ingredients. Soup is an excellent choice for dogs who for any number of reasons—old age, disease, hot summer weather—need to increase their intake of fluids.

BASIC DOG BROTH

2 pounds meaty beef bones
½ cup water
1 cup chopped onions
1 cup chopped celery
1 cup chopped carrots
¼ cup tomato paste
3 sprigs Italian parsley
1 teaspoon salt
3 black peppercorns
2 quarts water

Preheat oven to 350° F.

Place bones in a large roasting pan and roast them 1 hour, turning once or twice to brown on all sides. Drain off fat. Place roaster on stove-top burner over medium heat. Add ½ cup water and deglaze pan, loosening all browned bits. Reserve deglazed drippings.

In a large Dutch oven or heavy kettle, heat oil over medium heat. Add onions, celery, and carrots; sauté until onions are translucent, stirring often. Add roasted bones, reserved pan drippings, tomato paste, parsley, salt, peppercorns, and 2 quarts water. Bring to a boil over high heat; reduce heat and simmer, covered, 2 hours.

To use as a broth, strain mixture, let cool to room temperature, and refrigerate. Skim off any fat from surface and either refrigerate or freeze.

For soup, remove the bones; pour broth and vegetables over kibbles. *Makes about 1½ quarts broth or 2½ quarts soup.*

A basic dog broth is essential to have on hand. The rich flavor will enhance many dishes such as stews and gravies, and, if the broth is not strained, it can be served with all its vegetables over kibble or other dried food.

Don't Leave Home Without It

For the peripatetic pooch, it's wise to travel with a current health certificate and rabies vaccination certificate. For reentry into the U.S., a rabies certificate is mandatory, and it's best to have with you all the other current vaccination certificates.

CHICKEN STOCK

The addition of canned chicken broth will enrich the flavor of this stock. However, if you prefer a lighter stock, use water instead.

4 tablespoons corn oil
2 pounds chicken necks and backs
1 large can (46 ounces) chicken broth or 2½ quarts water
2 cups chopped onion
1 cup chopped carrot
3 sprigs Italian parsley
1 quart water

In a large Dutch oven or heavy kettle, heat 2 tablespoons oil over medium heat. Add chicken pieces and brown on all sides. Remove chicken and reserve. Add ½ cup chicken broth to pan and deglaze it over medium heat, loosening and scraping up all browned bits. Add drippings to chicken; reserve.

In same pan, heat remaining 2 tablespoons oil over medium heat. Add onions and carrots; sauté until onions are translucent. Add reserved chicken and drippings, parsley, remaining chicken broth, and water; bring to a boil. Reduce heat and simmer stock, covered, 2 hours.

For stock, strain mixture, let cool to room temperature, and refrigerate. Remove and discard hard fat from surface of stock. Cover stock and use within several days or freeze in small portions for later use.

For soup, remove chicken parts and serve vegetables and broth over kibble or rice. *Makes about 2½ quarts stock or 3 quarts soup.*

DOG DUMPLINGS

2 tablespoons unsalted butter
1 onion, finely chopped
1 tablespoon chopped Italian parsley
2 cups finely chopped beef or chicken livers
¼ teaspoon marjoram
Salt
Freshly ground black pepper
1 cup dried bread crumbs
½ cup hot water
1 large egg, beaten
Chicken Stock (page 84), or Basic Dog Broth (page 83)

Melt butter in skillet over medium heat. Add onion and parsley and sauté 5 minutes longer, stirring often. Scrape mixture into a mixing bowl.

In a small bowl, moisten bread crumbs with about ½ cup hot tap water, or enough to make a paste. Work bread crumb mixture into liver and vegetables. Add egg, mix well, and cover; allow mixture to firm up 30 minutes.

Moisten your hands and form dumpling mixture into balls about 1 inch in diameter, or drop dumplings by teaspoons into about 2½ quarts boiling stock or broth and cook, uncovered, 30 minutes. *Makes about 36 dumplings.*

These dumplings are terrific served with their broth over kibble. I like the way they look when they're formed by hand into lovely symmetrical balls, but your pet will enjoy them just as much if you drop teaspoons of the dumpling mixture directly into the stock.

SALUKI'S SIGHT-SAVING SOUP

After a long day's coursing, what self-respecting sight-hound could resist this savory soup? The extra carrots provide vitamin A, essential for those midnight chases.

The saluki is one of the oldest breeds, dating back seven thousand years to the ancient Sumerian empire. Salukis were so revered in the land of the pharaohs that they were mummified after death and placed in the tombs of their owners along the Nile.

2 tablespoons unsalted butter
1 onion, finely chopped
2 cups thickly sliced unscraped carrots
½ cup uncooked rice
1 medium unpeeled potato, cut into ¼-inch slices
Pinch of dried marjoram
Pinch of dried thyme
Pinch of dried oregano
Pinch freshly ground white pepper
Salt
2 cups beef stock
1 cup milk

Melt butter in a heavy saucepan over medium heat. Add onion and carrots and sauté, stirring often, until onion is translucent. Add rice, potato, marjoram, thyme, oregano, pepper, salt, and broth. Add water, if necessary, to cover vegetables. Bring to a boil, reduce heat, and simmer soup, covered, 20 minutes, or until vegetables are tender.

Purée soup in blender or food processing and return to saucepan. Add milk and heat slowly over moderate heat until very hot; do not allow to boil. Serve soup over kibble and leftover cooked meat. *Makes 1½ quarts soup.*

LIVER LOVER'S SOUP

1 tablespoon vegetable oil
1 pound beef liver, trimmed of membrane and chopped very fine
1½ quarts Basic Dog Broth (page 83)
Salt
Freshly ground black pepper
1 cup heavy cream
1 to 2 tablespoons unbleached all-purpose flour (optional)
2 tablespoons chopped Italian parsley
Kibble (pages 73–80) or steamed white or brown rice

Heat oil in a saucepan over medium heat. Add liver and sauté 5 minutes, stirring often. Add broth and salt and pepper to taste, and bring to a boil. Reduce heat and simmer soup, covered, 30 minutes. Stir in cream, which can be mixed with flour if you prefer a thicker soup, and heat through. Serve in a deep bowl over kibble or rice. *Makes 2 quarts soup.*

This creamy soup will give any dog a new lease on life. If your dog happens to be on a low-calorie diet, substitute plain lowfat yogurt for the cream.

SCOTTISH SOUP

This is a hearty soup, suitable for all dogs, but devised specially for Scottish terriers whose heritage no doubt inculcates a craving for lamb, barley, and cabbage. For the highest nutritional value, use either whole-grain hulled barley or Scotch barley. Pearl barley is the least nutritious form of the grain, losing three-quarters of its protein and nearly all of its fiber in the refining process.

1 pound boneless lamb, cut into ½-inch pieces
1½ quarts water
¼ cup whole-grain hulled or Scotch barley
1 tablespoon soy sauce
3 black peppercorns
1 onion, chopped
2 carrots, coarsely chopped
1 stalk celery, thinly sliced
½ green cabbage, shredded
2 tablespoons chopped Italian parsley

Put lamb and water into soup kettle and bring to a boil. Add barley and soy sauce; reduce heat and simmer soup, uncovered, 45 minutes. Skim any scum from surface. Add onion, carrots, and celery and simmer 1 hour longer, adding cabbage for last 30 minutes of cooking. Serve in a deep bowl sprinkled with parsley. *Makes 2½ quarts soup.*

PHEBE'S WINTER DOGSOUP

2 pounds chicken gizzards and hearts or beef heart, coarsely chopped
2 cups whole-grain hulled or Scotch barley
Cut-up seasonal vegetables as available: carrots, onions, whole garlic cloves, cabbage, and
*   others*
1 teaspoon vegetable broth powder
2 quarts water
Kibble (pages 73–80)

Place meat, barley, vegetables, and broth powder in a large soup kettle; add the water and bring to a boil. Reduce heat and simmer soup, covered, 30 minutes. Serve hot over kibble. *Makes about 4 quarts soup.*

Variation: Phebe's Summer Dogsoup
Use seasonally available summer vegetables. Substitute bulgur for barley and do not add until soup is cooked. At that point, stir in bulgur and let soak until softened.

Phebe's owner, Erin, says, "Phebe knows just when I am cooking 'her' soup, and she takes a special interest in the process. I'm sure it is quite tasty, as Phebe does a sort of mazurka while smacking her lips when her dish is filled."

Chicken gizzards and hearts deliver, respectively, 91 and 84 grams of protein per pound. That's a higher amount than sirloin steak, and at a quarter of the cost.

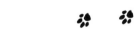

Vegetarian Dog Chowder

This recipe combines corn, an excellent source of vitamin A, and beans to provide a protein-rich chowder that your dog will find just as tasty as a meat-based dish.

2 medium unpeeled potatoes, cut into 1-inch cubes
3 cups water
2 tablespoons vegetable oil
1 clove garlic, minced
1 onion, coarsely chopped
4 cups fresh or frozen corn kernels
1 cup cooked kidney beans
1 cup milk
Pinch of freshly grated nutmeg
Salt
Freshly ground black pepper

In a small saucepan, combine potatoes and water and bring to a boil over medium heat. Reduce heat and cook potatoes until tender, 15 to 20 minutes. Drain potatoes, reserving cooking liquid and vegetable separately.

Heat oil in a large saucepan over medium heat. Add garlic and onion and sauté until onion is soft and translucent. Add corn and sauté 2 to 3 minutes longer. Stir in beans and reserved potato liquid and bring to a boil. Reduce heat and simmer soup, covered, for 5 to 8 minutes, or until corn is tender.

While soup is cooking, purée potatoes and milk in blender or food processor. Add to soup and heat through. Add nutmeg and salt and pepper to taste. Serve hot. *Makes 3 quarts soup.*

MAIN COURSES

Now you can offer your pet the same pleasure you accord yourself when you eat satisfying, well-prepared food. Your dog will discover a wonderful new mélange of textures, subtle scents, and delicious flavors from the main courses that follow. The pickiest of pooches will be intrigued by the variety of meats, poultry, and fish recipes. For the adventuresome dog, there are recipes that will transform the day's catch into a gourmet feast. Cosmopolitan dogs will revel in the internationally inspired mealtime possibilities, their taste whetted by the occasional doggy bag from a four-star people restaurant.

These main courses also offer practical, down-to-earth recipes that are good any time. Once your dog settles in with a few favorites, you may be tempted to feed him one dish exclusively. But to insure optimum nutrition, it is important to stay clear of culinary ruts. Be sure to serve a rich variety of foods in your pets' meal plan, and don't forget the vitamins.

PAVLOV'S DELIGHT

1 tablespoon unsalted butter
1 pound boneless beef chuck, cut into 1-inch pieces
2 cups beets, peeled and quartered
6 cups water
1 bay leaf
1 carrot, sliced
½ cabbage, shredded
Juice of 1 lemon
1 teaspoon vinegar
1 teaspoon sugar
Salt
Freshly ground black pepper
Kibble (pages 73–80)
Sour cream or yogurt for garnish

In a heavy soup kettle, melt butter over medium-high heat; add beef and brown on all sides. Add beets and water to pot and bring to a boil. Add bay leaf, reduce heat and simmer mixture, covered, 30 minutes. Remove kettle from heat.

Skim foam from soup, remove beets from kettle, and leave them at room temperature until cool enough to handle. Grate beets into kettle and add carrots, cabbage, lemon juice, vinegar, sugar, and salt to taste. Bring soup to a boil, reduce heat, and simmer 20 to 30 minutes longer. Remove bay leaf.

Put kibble in dog's bowl and ladle soup over it. Top with sour cream or yogurt and serve. *Makes 2½ quarts soup.*

In 1927 Ivan Petrovich Pavlov published the results of his famous experiment based on his concept of the conditioned reflex. While it was obvious that a dog would salivate in anticipation of food, Pavlov observed if food was presented simultaneously with the ringing of a bell, after a period of time the sound of the bell alone would cause the dog to salivate. Salivation in response to food is innate, an unconditioned reflex, but salivation in response to the ringing of a bell is acquired, or conditioned.

Even Pavlov was known to drool when pondering this succulent dish.

BOUVIER'S BEEF PIE

The Bouvier des Flandres, originally called *vuilbaard*, or "dirty beard," was developed by Flemish breeders as a cattle-herding dog. Bouviers were also used as ambulance dogs and messengers during World War I and, because so many of them were killed or abandoned during the bloody fighting in Flanders, the breed nearly disappeared. Fortunately, in the 1920s the few remaining bouviers were bred and the breed now flourishes.

2 tablespoons vegetable oil
8 ounces boneless beef chuck, cut into 1-inch cubes
8 ounces boneless veal shoulder, cut into 1-inch pieces
2 tablespoons unsalted butter
3 whites of leeks, well washed and cut into rounds
3 stalks celery, sliced
3 carrots, sliced
8 small white onions, peeled
1 tablespoon tamari sauce
1 tablespoon dry sherry
½ teaspoon dried thyme
Salt
Freshly ground black pepper
2 tablespoons chopped Italian parsley
½ cup Basic Dog Broth (page 83) mixed with 2 tablespoons cornstarch
Dough for double-crust 9-inch pie

Preheat oven to 350° F.

Heat oil in a large, heavy skillet over medium-high heat. Add beef and veal in batches and brown meat on all sides, transferring it to a bowl when browned.

Melt butter in same skillet. Add leeks, celery, carrots, and onions; sauté 5 to 8 minutes, or until vegetables are somewhat softened. Return meat to skillet with any juices that have accumulated and stir in tamari, sherry, thyme, and salt and pepper to taste. Remove skillet from heat and stir in parsley.

Roll out half the dough and line a deep 9-inch pie plate. Fill with meat and vegetable mixture. Stir broth and cornstarch mixture and pour over filling. Roll out remaining dough into a 10-inch round, place over top, and crimp edges. Cut a slit in center of crust. Bake 45 minutes, or until pastry is nicely browned. Cool 10 minutes before serving. *Makes one 9-inch deep-dish pie.*

Every dog has his day.
—Cervantes, *Don Quixote*

SCHNAUZER'S SCHNITZEL

Kibble (pages 73–80) or cooked egg noodles
2 pound boneless veal round, cut into thin strips
1 cup flour
2 egg yolks, beaten
1 cup dry bread crumbs
4 tablespoons (½ stick) unsalted butter
Dash of fresh lemon juice

In Renaissance Germany, schnauzers were so popular that artists frequently depicted them in paintings and drawings. It is said that Albrecht Dürer painted his pet schnauzer's portrait a number of times.

Put kibble or noodles in dog bowl.

Dredge veal in flour, then in egg yolks, then in bread crumbs. Melt butter in a heavy skillet; add veal in batches and brown on all sides, transferring pieces to dog bowl as they are browned. Sprinkle with lemon juice and serve. *Makes about 1 quart schnitzel.*

SUKIYAKI

Akitas were brought to the Japanese island of Honshu from China, where they were used to hunt deer, boar, and even bear. The Japanese regard the akita as a national treasure, and for this reason eventually forbade its use as a fighting dog. The akita has come into its own in the United States and Europe as a companion dog.

1 pound boneless round steak
2 ounces cellophane noodles (available in Oriental food shops)
1 chunk beef suet or 2 tablespoons vegetable oil
4 scallions, cut into 1-inch lengths
2 small onions, cut into quarters
1 cup mushrooms, cut into halves
1 cup bean sprouts
2 tablespoons soy sauce
1 teaspoon sugar
2 cups beef broth
4 to 8 ounces firm tofu, into 1-inch cubes
Steamed white rice

Freeze beef until firm enough to cut into very thin slices. Reserve.

In a kettle or large saucepan, bring 3 quarts water to a boil. Add noodles, reduce heat, and simmer, uncovered, 10 minutes, then drain and cut into 2- to 3-inch lengths. Reserve.

Place a large, heavy skillet or wok over high heat and rub bottom and sides with suet or brush with oil. Add scallions, onions, mushrooms, and bean sprouts; cook quickly, turning once, until soft. Move vegetables to side of skillet. Line bottom of skillet with sliced meat. Cook briefly on 1 side, sprinkle with soy sauce and sugar, and add 2 tablespoons of the broth.

Add cellophane noodles, tofu, and remaining broth; heat through, Place rice in dog's dish, arrange sukiyaki on top, and serve at once. *Makes 2 quarts sukiyaki.*

CANINE CHILI

2 tablespoons vegetable oil
1 pound lean ground beef
1 medium onion, chopped
1 green bell pepper, chopped
1 can (16 ounces) red kidney beans
1 can (6 ounces) tomato sauce
1 cup Chicken Stock (page 83)
Salt
Freshly ground black pepper
2 tablespoons chili powder
1 teaspoon ground cumin
¼ teaspoon ground cloves
Steamed rice or kibble (pages 73–80)

A mild chili that will appeal to most dogs, and particularly the Mexican hairless, a dog whose ancestors were the main ingredient in South American soups prior to the nineteenth century. Remember that dogs prefer blander fare than humans, so don't make their chili too spicy. Ordinary chili powder you can buy in a supermarket, used in the amount called for here, will be just spicy enough.

In a heavy skillet, heat vegetable oil over medium-high heat; add ground beef and brown it, breaking it up into small pieces with a wooden spoon. With a slotted spoon, transfer meat to a large saucepan.

Add onion and bell pepper to skillet and sauté over medium heat until onion is translucent, about 5 minutes. Add onion mixture to beef along with beans, tomato sauce, and chicken stock; mix well. Taste chili to see whether salt or pepper is needed. Add chili powder, cumin, and cloves with restraint, tasting as you stir them in a little at a time. After seasonings are added, simmer chili, covered, 45 minutes.

Serve chili over steamed rice or kibble. *Makes 1½ quarts chili.*

RUMANIAN DOG STEW WITH MEATBALLS

The vegetables and meatballs in this stew are enhanced by the rich flavor imparted by a large marrow bone, which should be discarded after cooking. Your dog will feast instead on vitamin-rich parsnips and carrots and delicate meatballs and won't miss gnawing on the forbidden bone.

1 marrow bone
2 quarts water
2 carrots, cut into 1-inch slices
1 parsnip, cut into 1-inch slices
1 tablespoon unsalted butter
2 onions, thickly sliced
2 large eggs
12 ounces ground beef
1 tablespoon bread crumbs
Salt
Freshly ground black pepper
Kibble (pages 73–80), toasted bread, or steamed grains
Yogurt
Chopped parsley

Place marrow bone in stock pot, add water, and bring to a boil over high heat. Reduce heat and simmer bone, covered, for 1½ hours, skimming foam from top from time to time. Add carrots and parsnip to pot and cook 30 minutes longer.

Melt butter in a skillet, add onions, and sauté over medium heat until onions are soft and translucent. Add onions to soup and cook about 15 minutes, or until the meatballs are prepared.

In a bowl, beat eggs lightly; add beef, bread crumbs, and salt and pepper to taste and combine well. Form mixture into 1-inch meatballs, drop them into soup, and simmer 45 minutes longer. Serve over kibble, toasted bread, or steamed grains. Top with yogurt, if desired, and sprinkle with parsley. *Makes 2½ quarts stew.*

How to Select a Kennel

1. A reputable kennel will allow an on-site inspection at any time and allow you to visit your dog at any time.
2. Each dog should have an indoor and outdoor area that is clean and odor free, with no accumulation of droppings. Runs should be at least 20 feet long.
3. An attendant should be available 24 hours a day, and a veterinarian should be on call at all hours.
4. The kennel should provide you with the brand of food served and substitute a diet of your choice, at your request.
5. Exercise outside of the run and human contact should be provided daily.

HARDY HOUND HASH

Some think the bloodhound's name came from its aristocratic bloodlines, which were kept pure by careful breeding in medieval monasteries. Others say the name honors the dog's hunting prowess—its highly developed sense of smell that allows it to zero in on wounded prey. The bloodhound is an amazing tracker and has been documented as following a man's scent for over 50 miles. One dog is said to have led detectives to their suspect after following the man's trail for 138 miles.

2 tablespoons unsalted butter
2 onions, finely chopped
¾ cup diced cooked potatoes
2 cups diced cooked beef
2 cups Basic Dog Broth (page 83)
1 tablespoon Worcestershire sauce
2 tablespoons tomato paste
1 cup fresh or frozen corn kernels
Salt
Freshly ground black pepper
1 pound fresh spinach, trimmed and well washed, or 1 package (10 ounces) frozen spinach, thawed

In a large, heavy skillet, melt butter over medium heat; add onions and sauté until soft and translucent. Stir in potatoes, beef, broth, Worcestershire sauce, and tomato paste; cook gently about 20 minutes. Mixture should be thick, but stirrable. Add corn and salt and pepper to taste during last 5 minutes of cooking.

Steam fresh spinach over boiling water just until limp or cook frozen spinach according to package instructions. Place spinach on dish and arrange hash on top. *Makes about 5 cups hash.*

"There's No Place Like Home" Steak, Kidney, and Kibble Pie

½ cup all-purpose flour
½ teaspoon dried marjoram
½ teaspoon dried thyme
Salt
Freshly ground black pepper
2 cups thinly sliced boneless round steak
1 cup 1-inch pieces beef, veal, or lamb kidney, trimmed of fat and membrane
Dough for 1-crust 9-inch pie
¾ cup kibble (pages 73–80)
1 tablespoon minced garlic
1 tablespoon prepared mustard
1 cup Basic Dog Broth (page 83)

Preheat oven to 350° F. and grease a deep 9-inch pie plate.

In a mixing bowl, combine flour, marjoram, thyme, and salt and pepper to taste. Add steak strips and kidney; toss to coat meats with seasoned flour. Shake off excess flour and transfer meat to baking dish. Add kibble. Mix garlic and mustard with stock and pour over meat and kibble.

Roll out dough into a 10-inch circle and fit it over top of pie plate. Crimp edges to seal tightly. Bake 25 to 30 minutes, until crust is crisp and browned. Let pie cool slightly and serve. *Makes one 9-inch deep-dish pie.*

Why do dogs just up and go?

- boredom
- lack of attention
- lack of love
- falling in love
- strong desire to play
- the call of the wild

When your dog returns from an unauthorized tour of the neighborhood, don't punish him; instead, offer devotion and affection and maybe a few Love Snaps (page 42).

MIXED MEATS LOAF

This dish is a cinch to prepare, and while it cooks your dog will revel in the subtle scents that fill the kitchen. Worcestershire sauce provides a special touch for dogs with a sophisticated palate.

1 large egg
½ cup minced onion
4 tablespoons chopped Italian parsley
½ cup rolled oats
1 cup chicken livers, chopped
12 ounces ground beef, veal, or pork
2 tablespoons Worcestershire sauce
2 tablespoons tomato paste
Salt
Freshly ground black pepper
½ cup dry bread crumbs
1 cup bulgur
1 cup water

Preheat oven to 325° F. and grease a large, shallow baking dish.

In a large mixing bowl, beat egg lightly; add onion, 2 tablespoons parsley, and oatmeal and mix well. Add chopped livers, ground meat, Worcestershire sauce, tomato paste, and salt and pepper to taste. Combine well with your hands to blend ingredients thoroughly. Form mixture into small loaves about 1½ to 2 inches in diameter and 4 to 6 inches long, place in baking dish, and sprinkle with bread crumbs. Bake 30 minutes.

While loaves bake, combine bulgur and water in small saucepan and bring to a boil over medium heat. Reduce heat, cover pan, and simmer 25 minutes.

Spread cooked bulgur on, arrange loaves on top, and sprinkle with remaining parsley. *Makes about 10 loaves.*

HUNGARIAN GOULASH

½ cup all-purpose flour
Salt
Freshly ground black pepper
1 pound boneless beef, cut into 1-inch cubes
1 pound boneless pork, cut into 1-inch cubes
2 tablespoons vegetable oil
½ cup chopped onion
2 cloves garlic, minced
1 tablespoon paprika
3 tablespoons tomato paste
3 cups Basic Dog Broth (page 83) or 1 cup broth and 2 cups water
½ cup sour cream
2 tablespoons chopped Italian parsley
Kibble (pages 73–80)

Combine flour and salt and pepper to taste. Dredge beef and pork in flour.

Heat oil in large, heavy skillet over medium-high heat. Add meat in batches and brown on all sides, adding more oil as necessary. Transfer browned meat to a bowl while remainder cooks. Return all browned meat and juices to skillet; add onion, garlic, paprika, tomato paste, and broth. Cover skillet and cook goulash over moderately low heat until meat is tender, about 1½ hours, adding water or broth as needed.

Ten minutes before serving, stir in sour cream and parsley. Serve on bed of kibble moistened with beef stock or water. *Makes 1½ quarts goulash.*

The puli is a Hungarian sheepdog with a dense undercoat of matted cords and a long, dark outer coat of tangles, which must be oiled and twisted as part of the grooming ritual. Pulik (the plural form), prized as herders, were easily spotted among the sheep, who, oddly enough, tend to mind a dark dog more readily than a light-colored one. A hardworking dog, the puli would stop at nothing to herd his flock, often running over the backs of the sheep to keep them in order. This hearty stew will rejuvenate the most exhausted sheepdog after a hard day's work.

SHEPHERD'S LAMB PIE

By the late nineteenth century, with wolves no longer menacing the European flocks and with the railroads being used to transport sheep, the Old World Shepherd was out of work, with few prospects. But German breeders believed that this beautiful and intelligent dog had potential for police work, and they began a vigorous breeding program that resulted in the German shepherd we know today. American soldiers returning from World War I brought German shepherds to the United States, where they were an immediate success. Since that time, the German shepherd has distinguished itself as a superb guard dog, police tracker, rescue dog, guide dog for the blind, and wartime hero.

1 pound ground lamb
4 medium all-purpose potatoes, peeled or unpeeled, sliced
1 cup green beans, cut into 1-inch pieces
4 tablespoons (½ stick) unsalted butter
1 onion, finely chopped
1 cup shelled fresh or frozen peas
1 cup fresh or frozen corn kernels
½ red bell pepper, finely chopped
½ teaspoon dried thyme
Salt
Freshly ground black pepper
¼ cup heavy cream
2 tablespoons chopped parsley
Paprika

Put lamb in a cold skillet, place over medium heat, and brown the meat, breaking it up into small pieces with a wooden spoon. Drain off fat and reserve lamb.

Put potatoes in a large steamer basket and steam over boiling water 20 minutes, or until tender. After potatoes have cooked 10 minutes, add green beans, keeping them separate from potatoes. When both vegetables are tender, put basket under cold running water long enough for vegetables to stop cooking. Reserve potatoes and green beans in separate bowls.

Preheat oven to 350° F. and butter a 2½-quart deep baking dish.

In a small skillet, melt 1 tablespoon butter over medium heat; add onion and sauté until translucent. Add peas, corn, bell pepper, cooked green beans, thyme, and salt and pepper to taste. Cook mixture 10 minutes over low heat, stirring often. Remove skillet from heat and stir in lamb, mixing it thoroughly into vegetables. Transfer mixture to baking dish.

In a small saucepan, melt 2 tablespoons butter; add cream and parsley and mix well. Pour mixture over potatoes and combine. Spread potatoes and their sauce over meat-vegetable mixture, dot top with remaining butter and sprinkle with paprika. Bake pie 30 minutes, or until top is golden brown. *Makes 2 quarts lamb pie.*

Dogs are great weather predictors and often become restless and whiny before thunderstorms.

The great pleasure of a dog is that you may make a fool of yourself with him and not only will he not scold you, but he will make a fool of himself too.
—Samuel Butler

TURNSPIT BARBECUE KEBABS

In England the turnspit was the canine equivalent of the galley slave; the dog turned the treadmills that rotated the spits that turned the meat over the roasting fires. If not locked in a cage, these unfortunate mongrels were tied to the wheel and worked for hours at a time just to cook a single roast. They understandably became resentful and were known for shirking their work at any opportunity.

Any dog, even a truculent turnspit, will appreciate these succulent lamb kebabs. Lamb delivers good-quality protein, but it is costly. For a more economical version, substitute chunks of beef. Whichever meat you serve, your dog will be delighted to be a guest at your summer barbecues.

8 small white onions, peeled
1/3 cup tomato paste
1 tablespoon Dijon mustard
1 tablespoon Worcestershire sauce
1/2 teaspoon dried oregano
Salt
1/4 cup dry white wine
1/4 cup white wine vinegar
2 tablespoons olive oil
4 pounds boneless lean leg of lamb, cut into 1½-inch cubes
3 zucchini, thickly sliced
Steamed rice

Place onions in a saucepan, cover with water, and bring to boil over medium heat. Boil onions gently 15 minutes. Drain and reserve.

To make the marinade: In a bowl, combine tomato paste, mustard, Worcestershire sauce, oregano, salt to taste, wine, vinegar, and olive oil, stirring to mix well.

Thread lamb, onions, and zucchini tightly on skewers. Place skewers in a shallow pan; pour marinade over skewers and let stand 1½ to 2 hours, turning skewers several times.

Broil on an outdoor grill or under a preheated broiler, turning frequently and basting with remaining marinade. Kebabs will be ready in about 15 to 20 minutes. Remove skewers before serving over rice. Leftovers are delicious served cold. *Makes 2 quarts kebabs.*

MUTTON-BARLEY STEW

1 quart Chicken Stock (page 83)
1 cup whole-grain hulled or Scotch barley
½ cup olive oil
2 pounds boneless lamb or mutton, cut into ½-inch cubes
3 cloves garlic, minced
2 tablespoons all-purpose flour
1 teaspoon dried rosemary
1 teaspoon dried oregano
Salt
Freshly ground black pepper
1 teaspoon soy sauce
1 teaspoon sherry
¼ cup chopped Italian parsley

Pour chicken stock into large soup kettle; add barley and bring to a boil. Reduce heat and simmer, uncovered, 30 minutes.

While barley cooks, heat olive oil in large skillet over medium heat. Add lamb in batches and brown on all sides, transferring browned pieces to a bowl. Sprinkle flour, rosemary, oregano, and salt and pepper to taste over lamb and toss to combine well. Add garlic to skillet and sauté 2 to 3 minutes. Ladle about ½ cup barley liquid into skillet and deglaze pan, scraping up browned bits. Add garlic mixture to lamb.

Transfer lamb mixture to soup kettle. Add soy sauce and sherry and stir to combine all ingredients. Simmer mixture 20 minutes longer, adding a little more flour dissolved in water if stew is not thick enough. Top with parsley. *Makes 3 quarts stew.*

This juicy, hearty mutton stew will fuel a hardworking sheepdog or any other large, active dog. In the old days, it was estimated that a good sheepdog could do the work of a dozen men. The job demanded that the dogs be intelligent and possess a great deal of stamina. On the move constantly, the average sheepdog covered at least four times more territory than traveled by the sheep it was guarding—a grueling job with little rest. The dogs' lunch breaks were spent preventing the sheep from bolting or wandering off, and at night they kept watch for wolves and other predators while the herdsman slept.

KERRY BLUE'S MULLIGAN STEW

Like the shamrock, the Kerry blue terrier is a symbol of Ireland, originating about one hundred years ago in County Kerry. A dog of all trades, the Kerry blue ably handles a variety of roles: water retriever, mouser, cattle dog, police dog, and children's nanny.

This stew, full of healthful vitamins, minerals, and fiber, will be all the more authentic if you can serve a freshly caught mouse on the side.

1 tablespoon vegetable oil
1 pound boneless lamb, cut into 1-inch cubes
1 quart water
1 cup chopped onion
2 cups diced carrots
1 cup diced potatoes
1 parsnip, diced
1 cup shredded cabbage
Salt
Freshly ground pepper
Kibble (pages 73–80)

Heat oil over medium heat in a Dutch oven or heavy kettle; add lamb and brown on all sides. Add water, onion, carrots, cabbage, potatoes, and parsnip and bring to a boil. Reduce heat and simmer stew, uncovered, 30 minutes. Add cabbage and salt and pepper to taste and cook until cabbage is tender, 10 to 15 minutes. Swirl in a scoop of kibble and serve. *Makes 2½ quarts stew (without kibble).*

SPICY AFGHAN'S YOGURT LAMB

4 tablespoons (½ stick) unsalted butter
1 onion, chopped
3 cloves garlic, minced
2 tomatoes, peeled, seeded, and chopped
1 tablespoon ground coriander
1 teaspoon ground cumin
½ teaspoon turmeric
½ teaspoon ground cardamom
¼ teaspoon ground cloves
Salt
Freshly ground black pepper
1 pound boneless lamb, cut into 1½-inch cubes
½ cup yogurt
Steamed white rice
2 tablespoons chopped fresh coriander

Melt butter in a large, heavy skillet over medium heat; add onion and garlic and sauté until onion is translucent. Add tomatoes, ground coriander, cumin, turmeric, cardamom, cloves, and salt and pepper to taste; sauté 2 to 3 minutes longer. Add lamb, increase heat to medium-high, and quickly brown meat on all sides.

Reduce heat to very low, slowly stir in yogurt, and cook, covered, 1 hour, adding a few tablespoons of water from time to time if mixture dries out.

Placed steamed rice in dog's dish, ladle stew on top, and sprinkle with chopped fresh coriander. Serve hot. *Makes 1 quart lamb stew.*

An ancient legend gives the Afghan credit for being the dog Noah selected to escape the great flood on his Ark. The elegant Afghan, although refined as a breed in Afghanistan, originated in ancient Egypt. Recorded on ancient papyrus over three thousand years ago and referred to as *cynocephalus*, or monkey-face, its picture is found in tombs in the Valley of the Nile. One of the great sighthunters, the Afghan is swift enough to hunt leopards, gazelles, and jackrabbits. Because its hipbones are wide-set and placed high on its back, the Afghan can handle rocky, uneven terrain, leap hurdles with ease, and turn on a dime.

Racetrack Ragoût

Until recently, professional racing greyhounds were unable to face their retirement years with any optimism. Because their racing careers are so short, these fleet, elegant dogs would find themselves washed up and ready for the doggie glue factory at the ripe old age of five. Happily, however, Retired Greyhounds as Pets (REGAP), a volunteer organization, has placed over several thousand retired greyhounds in approved homes.

This lovely lamb stew, redolent of wine, garlic, and bay leaf, will reward any dog—competitor or retiree.

1 pound shoulder lamb chops
2 tablespoons olive oil
3 medium onions, chopped
2 cloves garlic, minced
2 carrots, chopped
4 tomatoes, sliced, or 2 cups drained canned plum tomatoes
1 cup tomato purée
1 cup red wine
1 bay leaf
Salt
Freshly ground black pepper
Steamed rice

Trim fat from lamb chops and cut meat into bite-size pieces, leaving in bone. Heat oil in a large, heavy skillet over medium heat; add lamb and brown on all sides. Add onions, garlic, and 2 to 3 tablespoons water; continue cooking until onions are translucent. Reduce heat, add carrots and cook, uncovered, 15 minutes longer, adding water as needed to keep ingredients from scorching. Preheat oven to 350° F.

Add tomatoes, tomato puree, wine, and bay leaf, to lamb mixture in skillet; stir in salt and pepper to taste and combine well. Turn ragoût into a deep 2-quart casserole, cover, and bake 2 hours, adding water or wine as necessary.

Before serving, bone lamb and remove bay leaf. Serve ragoût over steamed rice. *Makes 2 quarts ragoût.*

JUNKYARD POT LUCK

1 onion, coarsely chopped
2 carrots, cut into ½-inch pieces
3 medium all-purpose potatoes, cut into ½-inch pieces
1 medium zucchini, cut into ½-inch pieces
8 ounces macaroni
2 cups cooked meat, cut into ½-inch pieces
1 can (16 ounces) kidney beans, drained
1 clove garlic, minced
1 cup Basic Dog Broth (page 83)
6 ounces tomato paste
1 tablespoon tamari sauce
½ teaspoon dried thyme
½ teaspoon dried oregano
Salt
Freshly ground black pepper

Place onion, carrots, potatoes, and zucchini in a steamer and steam vegetables over boiling water 15 to 20 minutes, or until potatoes are soft. While vegetables are steaming, cook macaroni according to package instructions; drain and reserve.

Place steamed vegetables in large saucepan. Add meat, kidney beans, garlic, and broth; stir well. Bring mixture to a simmer over medium heat and cook, until beans and meat are heated through, stirring frequently. Add tomato paste, tamari, thyme, oregano, salt and pepper to taste, and macaroni; simmer 20 minutes, adding more broth or water if mixture becomes too dry. *Makes about 3 quarts pot luck.*

This hearty dish can easily be assembled from refrigerator leftovers and is sure to warm the heart of the most stalwart guard dog.

*I'm a lean dog, a keen dog, a
   wild dog, and alone;
I'm a rough dog, a tough dog,
   hunting on my own;
I'm a bad dog, a mad dog,
   teasing silly sheep;
I love to sit and bay the moon,
   to keep fat souls from
   sleep.*
—Irene Rutherford McLeod,
   from "Lone Dog"

CANINE CARBONARA

This version of carbonara includes anchovies, a delicacy for dogs, who go wild over the fish aroma. You can easily improvise with the contents of this dish by including some of your family's leftovers in the ingredients. Presentation is all, and your dog won't guess he's eating secondhand food.

1 pound thickly sliced bacon, cut into 1-inch pieces
1 pound ziti
2 tablespoons olive oil
½ cup shelled fresh or frozen peas
1 onion, thinly sliced
½ cup mushrooms, cut into halves
5 anchovy fillets, drained
2 large eggs
½ cup freshly grated Parmesan cheese
Freshly ground black pepper

In a skillet, fry bacon over medium heat until crisp and brown. Drain bacon on paper towels and reserve. Discard bacon fat and wipe out skillet with paper towel.

In a large kettle, cook ziti according to package instructions. While pasta cooks, heat olive oil in skillet over medium-low heat. Add peas, onions, mushrooms, and anchovies; cook 10 minutes, stirring often.

Beat eggs in large bowl. Drain cooked pasta and toss with eggs in bowl until noodles are completely coated. Add bacon and vegetable-anchovy mixture and toss well. Sprinkle with Parmesan and pepper and serve at once. *Makes about 2½ quarts pasta.*

WELSH RAREBITE

3 tablespoons unsalted butter
2 cups sliced mushrooms
1 tablespoon all-purpose flour
1 cup milk
1 tablespoon Worcestershire sauce
1 tablespoon Dijon mustard
Salt
Freshly ground black pepper
1 cup diced cooked ham
1 cup shredded sharp Cheddar cheese
1½ cups Corn Kibble (page 76)

Melt 2 tablespoons butter in a small skillet over medium-high heat. Add mushrooms and sauté quickly, browning them slightly. Reserve.

Melt remaining butter in a heavy saucepan over medium low heat. Add flour and cook about 2 minutes, stirring constantly, until flour is barely golden. Gradually whisk milk into flour. When sauce has begun to thicken, add Worcestershire sauce, mustard, and salt and pepper to taste. If sauce seems too thick, add a little more milk to thin it.

Stir ham and mushrooms into sauce. Add half the cheese and mix until well combined. Put kibble in a dog bowl and pour cheese mixture over it. Sprinkle remaining cheese over top and serve. *Makes 1 quart rarebit and kibble.*

An Elegy on the Death of a Mad Dog

And in that town a dog was
  found,
As many dogs there be, Both
  mongrel, puppy, whelp, and
  hound,
and cur of low degree.

The dog, to gain some private
  ends,
Went mad, and bit the man.

The man recovered of the
  bite—
The dog it was that died.
—Oliver Goldsmith

BEAGLE'S BEANY CASSEROLE

The beagle is one of the oldest hounds in dog history. Its name derives from the French word *begle*, the dog used for chasing hare in the French countryside. Beagles have a reputation for being among the least fussy eaters in dogdom—they eat *anything!* How better to please than to serve your friend this savory pork and bean casserole enhanced by the rich flavor of molasses.

2 cups dried navy beans, picked over, rinsed, and soaked overnight
3 tablespoons vegetable oil
1 pound cooked pork, cut into small pieces
1 cup chopped onion
1 clove garlic, minced
3 carrots, coarsely chopped
1 cup tomato juice
2 tablespoons Dijon mustard
3 tablespoons dark molasses
1 teaspoon ground allspice
1 cup Basic Dog Broth (page 83)
Salt
Freshly ground black pepper

Drain and rinse beans and put in a large kettle with fresh water to cover. Bring to a boil over high heat, reduce heat, and simmer beans, covered, about 2 hours, or until tender. Check occasionally and add water as needed to keep beans from sticking.

Heat oil in a large skillet over medium heat; add pork and brown on all sides. Remove pork from skillet with slotted spoon and reserve. Add onion and garlic to skillet and sauté until onions are soft and translucent. Add carrots, tomato juice, mustard, molasses, and salt and pepper to taste and stir well. Simmer vegetables over very low heat, uncovered, 30 minutes, or until carrots are very tender, adding water if necessary. Stir broth and reserved pork into vegetables and simmer mixture 45 minutes, uncovered.

Preheat oven to 300° F.

Add meat and vegetables to beans, mixing well, and turn mixture into a 3-quart casserole. Cover and bake 2 hours. *Makes 2½ quarts.*

Note:

Beans may give some dogs flatulence. If doggy gas is a problem for your pooch, this dish should be fed sparingly.

The Nose Knows

- A dog's sense of smell is so well developed that the animal can distinguish between a set of identical twins.
- Dogs who are used to sniff out drugs can uncover marijuana or heroin disguised by multiple layers of odors.
- Dogs who are trained to scent out explosives can discover them twenty times faster than humans can.

RATATOUILLE WITH SAUSAGE

Rottweilers, descended from the herd dogs that drove cattle over the Alps for the armies of the Roman Empire, were developed as a breed in Rottweil, Germany, a central marketplace for the European livestock market. Because butchers, who carried large amounts of money, were frequently robbed by highway bandits, one enterprising butcher attached his money to his rottweiler's collar. Few robbers would risk tangling with these dedicated and powerful guard dogs, and so it became the custom for rottweilers to carry the butchers' money in transit.

½ cup olive oil
1 pound pork sausages, cut into 1-inch lengths
1 onion, quartered
2 cloves garlic, minced
1 small unpeeled eggplant, cut into 1-inch cubes
4 medium zucchini, sliced
4 tomatoes, cored and coarsely chopped
1 green bell pepper, cut into ½-inch squares
Bouquet garni: 1 tablespoon dried oregano, ½ teaspoon dried basil, ½ teaspoon marjoram,
*   and 2 or 3 peppercorns tied in a cheesecloth bag*
Salt
Freshly ground black pepper

In a large, heavy skillet, heat 2 tablespoons oil over medium heat; add sausages and begin to brown them. Stir in garlic and continue cooking until sausages are brown. Add remaining oil and heat it. Add garlic and sauté 2 to 3 minutes. Add eggplant, zucchini, tomatoes, bell pepper, bouquet garni, and salt and pepper to taste; continue to cook over medium heat until vegetables throw off their juices and mixture begins to simmer.

Reduce heat and simmer ratatouille, uncovered, until all the oil has been absorbed by the vegetables. Add water as needed to keep mixture from sticking to pan. Serve with chunks of dark, fresh-baked bread. *Makes 2½ to 3 quarts ratatouille.*

SAUSAGE AND RICE PILAF

2 tablespoons vegetable oil
1 pound breakfast sausages, casings removed
2 cups uncooked rice
½ cup chopped onion
1 cup shelled fresh or frozen peas
1 cup thickly sliced carrots
1 cup fresh or frozen corn kernels
1 quart Basic Dog Broth (page 83)
2 tablespoons tomato paste
Salt

Heat oil in a heavy skillet over medium heat. Add sausage and brown it, breaking up meat with wooden spoon or fork. Remove cooked meat with slotted spoon; reserve. Add rice and onion to skillet and cook, stirring, until onion is translucent and rice is opaque. Stir in peas, carrot, corn, cooked sausage, broth, and tomato paste. Season lightly with salt, cover skillet, and cook over moderately low heat until rice is tender, about 30 minutes, adding more broth if mixture dries out. *Makes 3 quarts pilaf.*

The keeshond got its name from Cornelius de Gyselaar, a member of the Dutch liberal Patriot Party who in the eighteenth century led a doomed revolt against the Prince of Orange, governor of the Netherlands. "Kees" is the Dutch nickname for Cornelius, and "hond" means dog, not hound. The spitzlike dog that was Cornelius' constant companion was therefore called "keeshond," or Cornelius' dog, and came to symbolize his cause. Until that time, the breed had been so well regarded that it appeared on the city seal of Amsterdam, but for a century thereafter the dog was tainted with the failure of the Patriot's revolt and only later regained its rightful popularity.

Hot Dogs Stuffed with Bacon and Potato

Say the words *hot dog* and the dachshund springs immediately to mind. Unknown outside Germany until the late nineteenth century, dachshunds come in three different hair styles: long, smooth, and wire-haired; and two different sizes: standard and miniature. The original dachshund hunted in packs for boar, foxes, rabbits, and especially badgers, but the breed was larger and heavier in those days, better suited to the task than today's domesticated dachshund. Here's a simple frankfurter recipe that will appeal to all dogs regardless of country of origin.

2 strips bacon
¼ cup chopped onion
1 cup mashed potatoes
Salt
Freshly ground black pepper
4 frankfurters, split lengthwise
½ cup shredded Cheddar cheese

Preheat oven to 350° F.

In a skillet, fry bacon over medium heat until crisp, drain on paper towels, and crumble. Add onion to skillet and sauté until translucent. Remove onions from skillet with a slotted spoon and place in mixing bowl. Add crumbled bacon, potatoes, and salt and pepper to taste. Mix well.

Fill frankfurters with potato mixture. Place on baking sheet, sprinkle tops with cheese, and bake 25 minutes. Let cool, then cut into bite-size pieces. *Makes 3½ cups frankfurter pieces.*

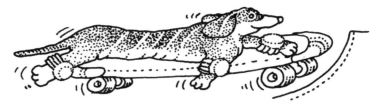

LION-HEARTED LASAGNA WITH LIVER

1 pound lasagna noodles
2 cups tomato sauce
1 clove garlic, minced
2 tablespoons fresh oregano leaves or 2 teaspoons dried oregano
2 tablespoons chopped fresh basil or 2 teaspoons dried basil
Salt
Freshly ground black pepper
1 cup chopped cooked chicken, beef, or calf's liver
2 cups ricotta cheese
8 ounces mozzarella cheese, shredded

In a large kettle, cook noodles according to package instructions. Drain noodles, rinse under cool running water, then drain again. Reserve noodles, covered.

In a heavy saucepan, combine tomato sauce, garlic, 1 tablespoon each fresh oregano and basil (or 1 teaspoon each dried), and salt and pepper to taste. Bring sauce to a simmer over medium heat; reduce heat and simmer sauce, covered, 30 minutes.

Preheat oven to 350° F.

Coat bottom of a 13 × 9-inch baking pan or lasagna pan with a thick layer of tomato sauce. Layer lasagna as follows: For base, 2 layers of noodles, then liver, ricotta, mozzarella, some of the remaining fresh herbs, and tomato sauce. For succeeding layers, use only a single layer of noodles. Top lasagna with a layer of sauce.

Cover pan tightly with foil and bake lasagna 30 minutes. Remove foil and bake 10 minutes longer. Remove pan from oven and allow lasagna to cool slightly before serving. *Makes 2 quarts lasagna.*

There actually is a lion dog, said to be one of the rarest of the purebreds. Called the little lion dog, it's a tiny pooch clipped to look like a lion, with a full mane and a plume at the end of the tail. The dog originated in Europe, and there is a lion dog in Goya's portrait of the Duchess of Alba. Sometimes weighing a mere 4½ pounds soaking wet, the lion dog has a winning personality and, though tiny, is courageous.

This protein- and fiber-packed lasagna will feed a whole pride of lion dogs, but it's easy to store in the refrigerator or freezer and re-heat in a moderate oven when ready to serve again.

LIVER ROLL-UPS

For many years, liver was a daily staple in the diet prepared by knowledgeable breeders. Today, some dog nutrition experts are concerned that liver on a daily basis may be harmful, due to toxic residues that accumulate in that organ. In moderation, however, liver is still an important source of nutrients.

Filling

1 cup diced cooked chicken livers or beef liver
1 small onion, cut in half
½ cup heavy cream
2 tablespoons chopped Italian parsley
½ cup dry bread crumbs
Salt
Freshly ground black pepper

Dough

1 cup all-purpose flour
1 teaspoon baking powder
Pinch of salt
2 tablespoons cold unsalted butter
½ cup cold milk

To make filling, chop livers fine in a food processor. Add onion, cream, parsley, bread crumbs, and salt and pepper to taste and process until mixture is of spreadable consistency.

Preheat oven to 450° F. and grease a baking sheet.

To make dough, sift flour, baking powder, and salt into a mixing bowl. Cut in butter with 2 knives or pastry blender. Stir in milk to make a soft dough on a lightly floured surface, roll out dough into a 12-inch square. Spread liver paste over dough and roll up.

Cut liver roll into 1-inch diagonal slices and place 1 inch apart on baking sheet. Bake 10 to 15 minutes. *Makes 10 to 12 roll-ups.*

COUSCOUS WITH CHICKEN LIVERS

1½ cups Chicken Stock (page 84)
1 cup couscous
4 tablespoons (½ stick) unsalted butter
8 ounces chicken livers, cut into small pieces
Salt
Freshly ground black pepper

In a small saucepan, bring 1 cup chicken stock to a boil. Remove pan from heat; stir in couscous and 2 tablespoons butter. Cover pan and let mixture stand for 10 minutes.

In a small skillet, melt remaining 2 tablespoons butter over medium heat. Add chicken livers and sauté until nicely browned on all sides.

Fluff up couscous with a fork and transfer to a dog bowl. Arrange chicken livers over couscous. Add remaining ½ cup chicken stock to skillet and deglaze pan over high heat, stirring up all the browned bits. Add salt and pepper to taste. Pour sauce over livers and couscous and serve. *Makes 3½ cups couscous.*

The sloughi, a descendent of the ancient royal Egyptian dogs, is relatively rare in the United States and Europe. But in North Africa the sloughi roams the deserts with nomadic tribes who prize the dog for its hunting skills and abilities as a guard dog. If you own a sloughi, the couscous in this dish will bring memories of its ancestral home; the aroma and flavor will suffice to make all other dogs sublimely happy.

FIREHOUSE SPECIAL

The dalmatian is the only breed in the world that naturally follows carriages, "coaching" under the axles. Its origins are thought to be in Dalmatia, but the breed's wide distribution is believed to result from its travel with the nomadic Romanies.

The dalmatian was valued for its sporting good looks and, as a coaching dog, for its affinity for horses. With the decline of coaching in the eighteenth century, the dalmatian found a new line of work at the firehouse, which perfectly suited its natural talents—a love of water, incredible stamina, and fleetness of foot.

This kidney dish requires only five minutes cooking time, a bonus for dogs who have to get out of the firehouse in a hurry.

6 lamb kidneys
½ cup all-purpose flour
Salt
Freshly ground black pepper
2 tablespoons olive oil
1 clove garlic, chopped
Kibble (pages 73–80) or steamed rice
1 tablespoon chopped parsley
Lemon wedge

Remove membranes from kidneys, slit them in half lengthwise, and remove white core. Cut kidneys into ½-inch pieces.

Combine flour and salt and pepper to taste. Dredge kidneys with seasoned flour. Heat oil in heavy skillet over medium heat; add kidney and garlic and sauté 4 to 5 minutes, stirring constantly.

Put kibble or rice in dog's bowl. Spoon kidneys on top, sprinkle with parsley, and spritz with lemon juice. *Makes 2 cups kidneys.*

CHEOPS CHICKEN

1 teaspoon ground cumin
1 teaspoon ground coriander
Salt
Freshly ground black pepper
1 chicken (3½ to 4 pounds), cut into 8 pieces
3 tablespoons olive oil
1 clove garlic, minced
1 onion, chopped
1 cup water
1 cup dry white wine
1 pinch of saffron
Steamed rice or couscous

Combine cumin, coriander, and salt and pepper to taste; rub mixture into chicken pieces.

Heat oil in a large, heavy skillet over medium-high heat. Add chicken and sauté, turning pieces until golden. Add garlic and onion; continue to sauté chicken until well browned on all sides. Add water, wine, and saffron and bring to a boil. Reduce heat, cover skillet, and cook chicken until tender, 45 to 60 minutes.

Remove bones from chicken. Make a bed of rice or couscous and arrange chicken on top. Pour gravy over chicken and serve. *Makes 1½ to 2 quarts chicken and gravy.*

The pharaoh hound is a sighthound specially bred for hunting. The dog probably originated in ancient Egypt, where paintings and carvings depict a dog very much like the modern-day pharaoh hound. The breed found its way to Spain and settled in the Balearic Islands. This recipe is made of succulent chicken simmered in exotic Mediterranean spices and wine—fit for a pharaoh or his dog.

GRAND PYRENEES PAELLA

The snowy great Pyrenees, or Patou (shepherd), was valued as a protector of flocks against wolves and bears. The breed developed in isolation in the harsh climate of the Pyrenees Mountains. Formidable and vigilant guard dogs, the Pyrenees was a favorite of peasants and royalty in the court of Louis XIV. Renowned as smugglers, these dogs were trained to carry contraband over the Franco-Spanish border, eluding customs officials by traveling dangerous mountain routes.

This paella is simpler than the version you might make for yourself, but it still requires a rich variety of ingredients. Since dogs have a supreme sense of smell, only a few precious threads of saffron are necessary for the maximum olfactory effect.

2 tablespoons olive oil
1 chicken (3 to 3½ pounds), cut into 8 pieces and boned*
1 clove garlic, minced
4 tomatoes, each cut into 6 to 8 wedges
1 red bell pepper, thinly sliced
6 cups Chicken Stock (page 84)
Salt
Freshly ground black pepper
2 cups uncooked rice
Pinch of saffron threads
1 cup shelled fresh or frozen peas
1 cup fresh shrimp, shelled and deveined
1 cup diced cooked ham

In a large, heavy skillet or Dutch oven, heat oil over medium-high heat. Add chicken and brown well on all sides. Add garlic, tomatoes, bell pepper, stock, and salt and pepper to taste; bring to a boil. Reduce heat and simmer mixture, uncovered, 20 minutes.

Slowly add rice, then stir in saffron and simmer paella, covered, 15 minutes. Add peas. Tuck shrimp and ham under rice and cook 5 to 10 minutes longer, until rice is tender and liquid is completely absorbed. Serve hot. *Makes 3½ quarts paella.*

*If you prefer to bone chicken after it is cooked, remove pieces from cooked paella and strip meat and skin from bones quickly with a fork and knife. Discard bones and return meat to paella.

SILENT STALKER'S STEW

1 chicken (3 to 3½ pounds), cut into 8 pieces
2 cups water
1 bay leaf
½ teaspoon dried oregano
½ teaspoon dried thyme
Salt
Freshly ground black pepper
8 ounces sausage links, cooked and cut into ½-inch lengths
3 potatoes, diced
2 carrots, cut into thick julienne strips
6 small white onions, peeled
1 cup Brussels sprouts, trimmed
1 quart Chicken Stock (page 84)
Kibble (pages 73–80)

Place chicken pieces in large kettle, add water, and bring to a boil over high heat. Reduce heat, add bay leaf, oregano, thyme, and salt and pepper to taste, and simmer chicken, covered, 25 minutes. Add sausage, potatoes, carrots, onions, and Brussels sprouts; continue to cook at a rapid simmer, covered, 20 minutes longer. Add some stock if mixture begins to dry out.

Remove chicken pieces and bone them. Arrange chicken and rest of stew over a plate of kibble. Pour enough stock over dish to make a rich gravy. Serve at once. *Makes 2½ to 3 quarts chicken stew.*

Basenjis are depicted in ancient Egyptian scrolls looking exactly as the breed does today. Eventually basenjis migrated further south in Africa, becoming silent stalkers for tribesmen in the Belgian Congo, where they were discovered by British explorers in the late nineteenth century. With an expressively wrinkled forehead, a tightly upcurled tail, and no bark at all, the basenji was immediately favored as an export. Fastidiously clean by nature, the basenji has a grooming ritual that is similar to a cat's and involves licking the entire coat to clean it. The basenji's chortle, described as an appealing yodel, is its most distinguishing characteristic.

This uncomplicated chicken and sausage stew can be frozen in pet-size portions.

SAVORY CHICKEN AND VEGETABLE PIE

This mild chicken pie is sure to soothe even the most pugnacious dog. If your dog is not likely to consume the whole pie in one sitting, cut it into individual slices and freeze it for future use.

2 tablespoons unsalted butter
1 onion, coarsely chopped
1 carrot, cut into ½-inch pieces
1 red bell pepper, cored, seeded, and cut into ½-inch pieces
3 medium unpeeled red potatoes, cut into ½-inch pieces
Kernels from 1 ear corn
1 cup Chicken Stock (page 84)
½ teaspoon dried thyme
½ teaspoon dried marjoram
Salt
Freshly ground black pepper
2 cups cut-up cooked boneless chicken (1-inch pieces)
2 tablespoons white wine
2 tablespoons cornstarch
Dough for double-crust 9-inch pie

Melt butter in a large skillet over medium heat. Add onion, carrot, bell pepper, potatoes, and corn, and sauté until onion is barely colored. Add ¼ cup chicken stock, thyme, marjoram, and salt and pepper to taste; simmer vegetables 20 minutes, stirring frequently. Stir chicken into vegetables and combine well.

Preheat oven to 325° F.

Roll out half the dough and line a 9-inch pie plate. Add chicken-vegetable mixture. Mix wine with cornstarch. Pour over chicken-vegetable mixture. Roll out remaining dough into a 10-inch round, place over top, and crimp edges. Cut a slit in center of crust. Place pie on a cookie sheet to catch the drippings and bake 45 minutes. Let cool before serving. *Makes one 9-inch pie.*

St. Bernard's Spring Chicken

1 large chicken (3½ to 4 pounds), cut into 8 pieces
6 cups Chicken Stock (page 84)
2 tablespoons unsalted butter
4 cooked unpeeled potatoes, thickly sliced
8 ounces bacon
4 slices bread, cut in half
4 tablespoons chopped parsley
Salt and pepper to taste

Place chicken in a large kettle, add stock, and bring to a boil. Reduce heat and simmer chicken, covered, 45 minutes, or until tender. Transfer chicken to dish and allow to cool. Reserve stock for another use.

Melt butter in a large skillet over medium heat; add potatoes and sauté until golden. In another skillet, fry bacon until crisp over medium-low heat. Drain bacon on paper towel, then break into small pieces. Add bread to bacon fat and fry over medium heat until browned on both sides.

Bone chicken, cut meat into bite-size pieces, and place in dog dish. Distribute potatoes, bread, and bacon around chicken. Sprinkle with parsley and serve. *Makes about 3½ quarts spring chicken.*

The St. Bernard takes its name from the Hospice at St. Bernard Pass in the Alps, where for over three hundred years monks trained St. Bernards to find lost travelers and to perform dangerous avalanche rescue work. It's estimated that over the years the St. Bernards saved more than 2,500 lives. Today the St. Bernard's job has been a casualty of progress; as the treacherous pass has been replaced by a tunnel, and trains go where once travelers journeyed on foot. The St. Bernard is a massive dog, often weighing in between 120 and 165 pounds. To keep up its strength, this burly dog requires an enormous amount of food—for instance, this delicious poached chicken with bacon and potatoes.

CHOW CHOW STIR-FRY

Chow-chow originally meant "mixed pickles" in pidgin-English and was the term used by traders to lump their cargo into one catchall category. The expression later came to include the aloof, leonine dogs that made their way from China to England in the eighteenth century. Among the most ancient of breeds, well established over two thousand years ago, the chow chow was used as a sporting dog, draft dog, guard, and as one of the dogs grown on special farms to feed the masses in Peking and Canton. Like the Pekingese, their fur was considered valuable and for this reason chows were included in many a bride's dowry.

The chow's unique stiff-legged gait, black tongue, and rich fur make this breed especially exotic.

1 teaspoon brown bean sauce
2 teaspoons tamari sauce
½ cup Chicken Stock (page 84)
1 teaspoon cornstarch
2 tablespoons vegetable oil
1 cup cut-up boneless chicken (½-inch pieces)
3 carrots, thinly sliced on diagonal
2 stalks celery, thinly sliced on diagonal
2 scallions, sliced
1 cup tofu, cut into 1-inch cubes
Steamed rice

Blend brown bean sauce, tamari sauce, stock, and cornstarch; reserve. Heat 1 tablespoon oil in a wok or heavy skillet over medium-high heat. Add chicken and quickly stir-fry until it is no longer pink. Remove from wok with slotted spoon and reserve. Add remaining 1 tablespoon oil to wok and heat. When hot, add carrots and celery and stir-fry until crisp-tender, about 5 minutes. Add tamari mixture and chicken and stir-fry 2 minutes longer. Add scallions and tofu and stir-fry until tofu is heated through and coated with sauce. Serve over rice. *Makes about 1 quart chicken and vegetables.*

CATAHOULA GUMBO

2 tablespoons olive oil
1 chicken (3 to 3½ pounds), cut into 8 pieces
1 onion, coarsely chopped
1 clove garlic, minced
1 cup diced smoked ham
1 cup diced okra, fresh, frozen or canned
¼ cup tomato paste
6 cups water
1 bay leaf
Pinch of cayenne pepper
1 tablespoon Worcestershire sauce
Salt
Freshly ground black pepper
1 pound fresh shrimp, shelled and deveined
Steamed white rice

Heat oil in a large, heavy kettle over medium-high heat. Add chicken and brown well on all sides. Add onion and garlic and sauté over medium heat 10 minutes, stirring often. Add ham, okra, tomato paste, water, bay leaf, cayenne, Worcestershire sauce, and salt and pepper to taste. Bring gumbo to a boil, reduce heat, and simmer, covered, 1 hour. Add shrimp and cook 15 minutes more. Remove chicken pieces and bone them, returning meat to gumbo. Discard bay leaf. Spoon rice into dog dish and top with gumbo. Serve hot. *Makes 2½ to 3 quarts gumbo.*

The Catahoula leopard dog arrived in Louisiana with the first colonists from France to settle in the Catahoula parish. This dog is used to herd livestock, hunt raccoons, and serve as a top-notch guard dog. Speckled unevenly (hence the name), this long, lean, short-haired dog is occasionally found with brilliant turquoise eyes.

Catahoula Gumbo will have your dog dreaming of either a romp through steamy bayous, if that's his inclination, or perhaps of a relaxing afternoon stretched out beneath the sweet blossoms of a magnolia tree. Use a light hand with the cayenne so as not to overwhelm your pet's sensitive canine nose.

TERRIER'S TERRIFIC TURKEY BURGERS

Fox terriers are born with about four times as much original sin in them as other dogs.
—Jerome K. Jerome,
 Three Men in a Boat

8 ounces boneless, skinless turkey meat, cut into small pieces
½ cup half-and-half
¼ cup finely chopped onion
½ cup dried bread crumbs
Salt
Freshly ground black pepper
3 tablespoons olive oil
1 tablespoon unsalted butter
½ cup Chicken Stock (page 84)
1 tablespoon chopped Italian parsley
Sliced bread

Put turkey in food processor, add 2 to 3 tablespoons half-and-half, and process until turkey is coarsely chopped; add more half-and-half if needed, but keep the mixture thick. Transfer turkey to a mixing bowl. Add onion, bread crumbs, remaining half-and-half, and salt and pepper to taste; combine mixture thoroughly. Shape into 4 patties, each 3 inches in diameter.

Heat 2 tablespoons olive oil in heavy skillet over medium heat. Add patties and sauté about 5 minutes on each side, or until patties are cooked through.

Meanwhile, in small saucepan, heat remaining olive oil, the butter, stock, and parsley over medium heat until butter melts. Place a slice of bread in dog dish, arrange a turkey burger on top (cut into bite-sized pieces, if necessary), and pour sauce over all. *Makes 4 turkey burgers.*

SPANIEL SOUFFLÉ À LA KING

4 tablespoons (½ stick) unsalted butter
2 tablespoons all-purpose unbleached flour
½ teaspoon salt
1 cup milk
3 large eggs, separated
½ cup bread crumbs
1 teaspoon lemon juice
¼ teaspoon freshly ground white or black pepper
½ teaspoon paprika
1 teaspoon chopped Italian parsley
2 cups chopped cooked turkey

Preheat oven to 350° F. and grease a 1½-quart soufflé dish.

Melt butter in a saucepan, over low heat; stir in flour and salt and cook until a paste forms. Add milk, stirring constantly with a whisk, and cook until sauce is very thick. Remove pan from heat. While sauce is still very hot, add egg yolks, one at a time, whisking vigorously after each addition. Add bread crumbs, lemon juice, pepper, paprika, parsley, and turkey and mix well.

In mixing bowl, beat egg whites until they hold stiff peaks. Stir one-third of whites into turkey mixture. Fold in remaining whites and spoon mixture into soufflé dish. Bake 20 to 25 minutes, or until firm. Serve at once. *Makes one 2-quart soufflé.*

The King Charles spaniel migrated from China, via Japan and Spain, to England, where the tiny spaniel immediately became a royal favorite. Legend has it that the devoted pet of Mary Queen of Scots followed her up the scaffold as she was led to her death in 1567. The breed was finally named after the famous royal roué, King Charles II.

Nothing makes a dog feel more civilized and regal than a freshly baked soufflé, hot from the oven. The soufflé provides your pet with a new and appealing texture, much lighter than the usual crunchy fare. This high-protein dish can be served on special occasions.

COONHOUND PIE

Coonhounds are slow and steady trackers, and they trail with their noses to the ground. Once the dog has treed his coon, he begins to "bark up," a distinctive baying sound. Coonhounds are also adept at tracking deer, bear, and mountain lions.

For the sake of authenticity, it would be best to have a freshly caught raccoon on hand when making this recipe. But authenticity isn't everything in life, and rabbit makes an acceptable substitute.

1 small rabbit (about 2½ pounds), thawed if frozen, cut into 8 pieces
1 cup all-purpose flour
Salt
Freshly ground black pepper
4 tablespoons (½ stick) unsalted butter
1 onion, coarsely chopped
4 medium all-purpose potatoes, peeled and coarsely chopped
1 pound fresh okra, sliced, or 1 box (10 ounces) frozen sliced okra, thawed
1 cup shelled fresh or frozen peas
Dough for double-crust 9-inch pie
2 tablespoons tomato paste
¾ cup Chicken Stock (page 84)
1 tablespoon tamari sauce

Wash and bone rabbit, using a sharp, thin knife. Cut the meat into bite-size pieces. Combine flour with salt and pepper to taste, and dredge rabbit meat in mixture. Melt butter in a large, heavy skillet over medium heat; add rabbit and brown pieces on all sides. Remove rabbit to a plate and reserve.

Add onion, potatoes, and okra to drippings in skillet, stirring to loosen all the browned bits. Cook vegetables over medium heat until tender, adding water if necessary to keep them from sticking and stirring mixture often. Add browned rabbit, peas, and salt and pepper to taste.

Preheat oven to 350° F.

Roll out a little less than half the dough and line a 9-inch pie plate. Transfer rabbit-vegetable mixture to pie plate. In a small bowl, mix tomato paste, stock, and tamari and pour over the meat and vegetables.

Roll out remaining dough into a 10-inch round, place it over top, and crimp edges decoratively. Cut slit in top crust. Place pie on a cookie sheet to catch the drippings, and bake 45 minutes. *Makes one 9-inch pie.*

Bone Appétit! safety tip: *Never* attempt to get between fighting dogs. Douse them with water or use a broomstick to restore order. If you can do it without getting bitten, pull the underdog away by his tail.

ROAST STUFFED RABBIT

The whippet is comparatively new to the sighthound family, originating in England just one hundred years ago. "Whip-it" was a slang expression for running. Capable of reaching 35 miles per hour, the whippet combines the speed of the greyhound with the ratting instincts of the terrier—characteristics that make this breed a superior rabbit dog. What better reward for your pet than this simple roast rabbit with heady sage stuffing.

1 whole, cleaned rabbit
1 orange, cut in half
Salt
Freshly ground black pepper
2 cups dried bread cubes
2 tablespoons chopped onion
2 tablespoons chopped Italian parsley
1 teaspoon dried sage
4 tablespoons (½ stick) unsalted butter, melted

Wash rabbit thoroughly and pat dry. Rub it well inside and out with cut sides of orange and sprinkle inside with salt and pepper to taste.

Preheat oven to 350° F.

In a mixing bowl, gently combine bread, onion, parsley, sage, salt and pepper to taste, and 2 tablespoons butter. Stuff rabbit with mixture, then sew up opening.

Place rabbit in roasting pan, brush with remaining melted butter, and roast, uncovered, for 1½ hours, or until tender. Cut rabbit meat from bone and serve with stuffing. *Makes 4 medium servings.*

POODLE POLENTA

½ teaspoon salt
1 cup cornmeal
1 cup milk
¼ teaspoon freshly ground black pepper
1½ cups freshly grated Parmesan cheese

Bring water to a boil in bottom of double boiler. In top of double boiler, over direct heat, bring 2 cups water and the salt to a boil. Add cornmeal slowly, stirring constantly with a wooden spoon. Remove pan from heat and set over the boiling water. Add milk and pepper and cook, covered, over boiling water 30 minutes, stirring occasionally. Stir in 1 cup cheese and remove from heat.

Moisten a flat dish with cold water, spread out cornmeal mixture on it, and allow to cool.

Preheat oven to 400° F. and grease a baking sheet.

Cut polenta into 2-inch squares and place on baking sheet. Sprinkle remaining cheese over polenta and bake until cheese is melted and lightly browned, about 10 minutes. *Makes 18 polenta squares.*

This simple recipe is reminiscent of the Italian maize flour dish.

Jet Setters
Most airlines will allow a dog in the cabin if the kennel can be squeezed under the seat (maximum height, 8 inches). The catch is that no other carry-on luggage is permitted and the invitation does not extend to commuter flights. Of course, seeing-eye dogs in harness are permitted in the cabin.

Sheltie Potato Stew

The ancestors of the miniature collie, or Shetland sheepdog, were brought over to the Shetland Islands from mainland Scotland and crossed with smaller breeds to produce the Sheltie as we know it today. Life in the Shetland Islands is harsh and rugged, shaped by the cold sea and frequent storms. The land is rocky, the vegetation scrubby and sparse. Toughened by this rough environment, the Sheltie's miniaturization was in part due to the climate. Many herding dogs were sustained in these islands, as well as in Ireland and Scotland, with nothing more than a hearty gruel of potatoes and milk, which was shared with their masters. Here's a simple potato stew, with egg added for higher protein.

8 large white potatoes
2 tablespoons unsalted butter
2 tablespoons cornstarch
1½ cups milk
Salt
Freshly ground white or black pepper
2 hard-cooked eggs, coarsely chopped
2 tablespoons chopped Italian parsley

Wash and scrub potatoes, put in a large saucepan with cold water to cover, and bring to a boil over high heat. Boil potatoes for 30 minutes, or until tender, then drain and keep warm.

Melt butter over low heat in a small saucepan; add cornstarch and cook, stirring, until cornstarch is barely golden. Stir in milk gradually, whisking constantly, and cook until sauce is thickened. Add salt and pepper to taste.

Cut potatoes into bite-size pieces and put in a bowl. Add chopped eggs, parsley, and sauce; toss to mix well. Serve hot. *Makes 1½ quarts stew.*

FISH BISQUE

2 tablespoons unsalted butter
1 onion, chopped
1 carrot, chopped
1 tablespoon chopped parsley
½ teaspoon dried thyme
1 bay leaf
8 ounces boneless white fish, cut into 1½-inch pieces
4 ounces shellfish (shelled scallops, crabmeat, or shrimp)
2 cups fish stock
Salt
Freshly ground white pepper
1 tablespoon cornstarch dissolved in 2 tablespoons cold water
1 cup heavy cream
¼ cup white wine
Kibble (pages 73–80), steamed rice, or pieces of hand-torn French bread

Melt butter over medium heat in a large saucepan. Add onion, carrot, parsley, thyme, and bay leaf; sauté until onion is translucent. Add fish, shellfish, fish stock, and salt and pepper to taste; bring to a simmer. Simmer mixture, covered, for 6 to 10 minutes. Add cornstarch mixture and cook, stirring constantly, until bisque is thickened. Add cream and wine and heat through. Serve immediately over kibble, rice, or bread. *Makes 1½ quarts bisque.*

This luxurious bisque, a once-a-year treat for your privileged pet, provides plenty of high-protein fish and luscious flavor.

Beauty without Vanity, Strength without Insolence, Courage without Ferocity, and all the Virtues of Man, without his Vices.
—Lord Byron, from an inscription on the monument to the memory of Boatswain, a Newfoundland

HOT OPEN-FACED SARDINE SANDWICHES

Sardines are an excellent source of calcium and protein and practical to carry while traveling. Toy dogs love these delicate hot sandwiches.

3 slices bread
Mayonnaise
Dijon mustard
1 can sardines with bones, drained
½ onion, minced
⅓ cup grated Cheddar, Jarlsberg, or Muenster cheese
Dash paprika

Preheat broiler. Toast bread. Spread one side of each slice with mayonnaise and mustard. Arrange sardines over toast. Sprinkle with onion and cheese and heat under broiler until cheese is melted. Cut into bite-size pieces and serve. *Makes 3 sandwiches.*

PROVENÇAL FISH STEW

3 tablespoons olive oil
2 onions, chopped
1 clove garlic, minced
4 potatoes, each cut into eighths
3 tomatoes, sliced
1½ quarts fish stock
10 mussels, steamed, shelled, and juices reserved
2 pounds turbot or flounder fillets, cut into 1½-inch pieces
10 shrimp, shelled and deveined
Juice of 1 lemon
Salt
Freshly ground black pepper
2 tablespoons chopped Italian parsley

Heat olive oil in large, heavy saucepan over medium heat. Add onions and garlic and sauté until onion is translucent. Add potatoes and cook 15 minutes longer, adding water if necessary to keep potatoes from sticking to pan. Add tomatoes, fish stock, mussel juices, turbot or flounder, and shrimp; cook about 5 minutes, or until turbot and shrimp are just cooked through. Stir in the mussels 2 minutes before end of cooking. Add lemon juice and salt and pepper to taste. Serve hot, sprinkled with parsley. *Makes 3 quarts stew.*

In the south of France, there is a water spaniel known as the Épagneul de Pont-Audemère, named after the river Aude. The Pont-Audemère is a great lover of water and of course thrives on this succulent fish stew.

Canine Careers

- herder
- guard
- guide for the blind or hearing impaired
- animal hunter
- tracker
- police dog, sniffing out explosives, drugs, and criminals
- in wartime, a bearer of medicine and a rescuer of wounded soldiers
- space explorer
- circus performer
- racer
- movie and TV actor
- model
- fighter
- man's best friend

Dogs selected to work as guides must have the intelligence of a seven-year-old child and be able to respond to a large number of verbal commands. Temperament is the most essential ingredient, and potential guide dogs must be friendly, adaptable, even tempered, calm, tolerant of crowds and noise, and unaffected by the difficulties of various kinds of transportation. Perhaps most important, a guide dog must learn strict obedience, yet be able to exhibit "intelligent disobedience" in order to insure the safety of its master.

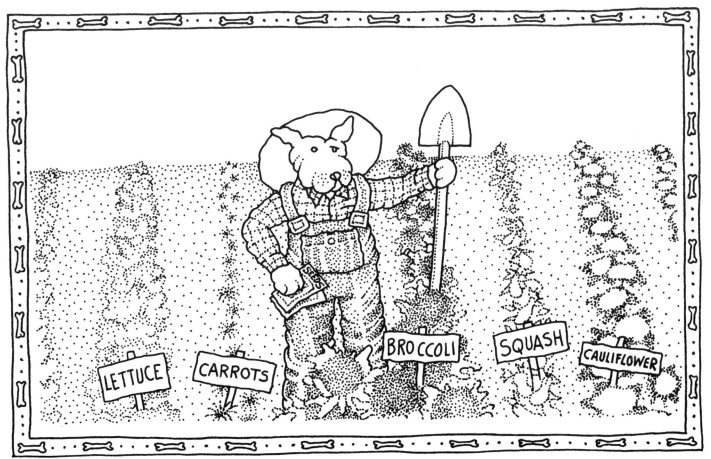

VEGETABLES

Many people are surprised to learn that dogs really love vegetables, which provide a rare treat for those unfortunate creatures who know little other than canned and kibbled monotony day after day. The wonderful texture and crunch of fresh, juicy vegetables are important in the canine diet—both for gastronomic pleasure and nutritional benefits.

STEAMED BROCCOLI WITH CHEESE SAUCE

Stems from 1 bunch broccoli
2 tablespoons unsalted butter
2 tablespoons all-purpose flour
1 cup milk
1 cup grated Cheddar cheese
Salt
Freshly ground black pepper
Steamed rice

Use a sharp paring knife to peel skins from broccoli stems. Cut stems into bite-size pieces and place in steamer. Steam broccoli, covered, over boiling water until just tender. The vegetable should be a bright, fresh green.

While broccoli is cooking, melt butter in small saucepan over medium-low heat; stir in flour and cook until mixture is golden. Do not allow roux to brown. Add milk slowly, stirring constantly. Add cheese and stir until melted. Add salt and pepper to taste.

Make a bed of rice in dog dish, top with broccoli, and pour on sauce. *Makes 3 cups vegetable and sauce.*

Dogs usually aren't too picky about which part of broccoli they eat. For this reason, it's economical to save the tender florets for yourself and serve the stems to your dog in this delicious main course. The slightly tougher stems are an excellent source of roughage as well as of protein, which is augmented by the cheese.

POTATO PANCAKES

When preparing potatoes for your dog, it is not necessary to peel them, but you must remove any sprouting buds because they contain a toxic substance.

5 medium potatoes
Salt
1 cup milk
3 large eggs, separated
4 tablespoons (½ stick) unsalted butter
Yogurt, cottage cheese, or sour cream

Put potatoes in a saucepan with salted water to cover, bring to a boil over high heat, and cook until tender, 25 to 30 minutes. Drain potatoes and mash with their skins, then stir in milk and egg yolks, beating well. In mixing bowl, beat egg whites until stiff, then fold into potatoes.

Melt 1 to 2 tablespoons butter on a griddle over medium heat. Drop 1 tablespoon potato mixture on griddle for each pancake and cook pancakes until lightly browned on both sides. Continue making pancakes, adding more butter to griddle as needed. Serve with yogurt, cottage cheese, or sour cream. *Makes about 42 three-inch pancakes.*

BIG RED'S POTATOES AU GRATIN

10 red Bliss potatoes, thinly sliced
1 cup ricotta cheese
1 cup grated Jarlsberg cheese
1 cup milk
1 large egg
3 tablespoons unsalted butter, melted
½ cup chopped parsley
Salt
Freshly ground black pepper

Preheat oven to 325° F. and grease a 2-quart baking dish.

Bring a large saucepan of water to a boil. Add potatoes and boil 5 minutes, then drain and rinse with cold water.

In prepared baking dish, alternate layers of potatoes, ricotta, and Jarlsberg. In a mixing blow, beat together milk, egg, parsley, and salt and pepper to taste. Pour milk mixture over potato-cheese layers and bake 45 minutes, or until potatoes are tender and top is well browned. *Makes 1¾ quarts potatoes.*

This is a hearty dish that will appeal to both sporting and pampered dogs. The Irish setter perfectly fits both descriptions. Blessed with great beauty, the glossy Irish setter has begun to predominate as a show dog, and its stamina and loyalty in the field have been somewhat overlooked in recent years. A late bloomer and a natural clown, setters can be difficult to train, but it's said that the lessons, once learned, will last throughout its long lifetime.

In this recipe the combination of potatoes and cheese provides a hearty change of pace along with plenty of vitamins C and B. Dogs who must tolerate extremes of temperature actually need more B complex vitamins in their diet.

BAKED POTATOES WITH CHEESE AND MEAT STUFFING

These tasty stuffed baked potatoes are filling enough to satisfy the giant breeds, among them the shaggy Irish wolfhound, weighing in at over 100 pounds. A superb hunter, the breed has stalked lion on safari in Africa and coyotes, timber wolves, and elk on other continents. By now, of course, the Irish wolfhound is a docile and devoted companion, content to dine on domestic fare.

2 large Idaho baking potatoes
8 ounces ground beef, pork, or lamb
Salt
Freshly ground black pepper
1 cup grated Muenster cheese
2 tablespoons Worcestershire sauce
2 teaspoons chopped fresh chives or green top of scallions

Preheat oven to 425° F.

Scrub potatoes, pierce skin with tines of fork, wrap in foil and bake 45 to 60 minutes, or until tender when pierced.

While potatoes are baking, place meat in a cold skillet and cook over medium heat, breaking up meat with a wooden spoon until no longer pink. Add salt and pepper to taste and drain off any fat that has accumulated in pan. Scrape meat into a mixing bowl.

Split potatoes in half lengthwise and scoop pulp into bowl with meat. Add cheese and Worcestershire sauce; mix well. Pile filling into potato shells, place potatoes on a baking sheet and bake 20 minutes, or until cheese is melted. Sprinkle with chives and serve. *Makes 4 stuffed potato halves.*

CREAMY SWEET POTATOES

3 large sweet potatoes
3 tablespoons unsalted butter
½ cup heavy cream
Salt
Freshly ground black pepper
Pinch of freshly grated nutmeg

Preheat oven to 350° F.

Scrub potatoes, prick them on top with a fork, wrap in foil, and bake 1½ hours, or until soft.

Just before potatoes are done, melt butter in a small saucepan over medium-low heat. Add cream, salt and pepper to taste, and nutmeg, and heat through without boiling. Keep sauce warm.

Slice potatoes into rounds, cutting through bottom skin. Put potato slices in a bowl, pour sauce over them, and toss gently. *Makes 3 cups sweet potatoes.*

Most dogs love sweet potatoes, skins and all. Nutritionally, sweet potatoes provide fiber and potassium, as do white potatoes, and they also have an astonishingly large amount of vitamins A and C. Yams can be substituted if sweet potatoes are not available.

BAKED SQUASH

This is an excellent meal for your dog—simple to prepare and very tasty. In winter, acorn squash is an economical fresh vegetable that is full of nutrients and rich in vitamin A, essential for a lustrous coat.

2 acorn squash
2 tablespoons unsalted butter
½ teaspoon ground allspice

Preheat oven to 350° F.

Cut squash in half and scoop out seeds and stringy membranes. Place squash halves, cut sides up, in center of an oblong baking dish containing 1 inch water. Place ½ tablespoon butter in each squash half and sprinkle with allspice. Cover squash with foil and bake 1 hour, or until tender. Cut squash, with skins into bite-size pieces and serve. *Makes 3 cups squash.*

STUFFED ZUCCHINI

6 medium zucchini
1 cup grated Jarlsberg cheese
½ cup dried bread crumbs
½ cup sliced onion
2 tablespoons chopped Italian parsley
Salt
Freshly ground black pepper

Place whole zucchini in a large saucepan, cover with water, and bring to a boil over high heat. Reduce heat and cook zucchini at a slow boil 20 minutes. Drain zucchini and place in a bowl of ice water to cool.

Preheat oven to 350° F. and butter a shallow baking dish large enough to accommodate the zucchini in one layer.

Slice zucchini lengthwise and scoop out pulp with a small spoon or melon ball cutter. Chop pulp coarsely and place in a mixing bowl. Add cheese, onion, bread crumbs, and parsley; mix well. Add salt and pepper to taste.

Place zucchini shells in baking dish, divide filling among zucchini, and bake, uncovered, 20 minutes, or until filling is hot, cheese is melted, and top is lightly browned. Allow to cool slightly, then cut into bite-size pieces and serve with potatoes or rice. *Makes about 1 quart stuffed zucchini.*

In mid-nineteenth century Edinburgh, Auld Jock and his Skye terrier, Greyfriars Bobby, were inseparable during life. When Auld Jock died and was buried in the town cemetery, Greyfriars Bobby stayed with him and kept vigil at his grave for ten years. Touched by the dog's devotion, the townspeople fed him and later erected a statue in his honor.

ZUCCHINI WITH OYSTER SAUCE

Oyster sauce is irresistible to most dogs and cats, and it transforms this simple but delicious vegetable dish into a satisfying main course. Oyster sauce can be bought at all Oriental food stores and in an increasing number of supermarkets.

Zucchini is economical, easy to digest, delicious, and available year-round. Dogs like its texture, and if you should find yourself with a surfeit of zucchini in the garden, you might consider using it in a number of your pet's summer meals.

½ cup Chicken Stock (page 84)
2 tablespoons oyster sauce
1 tablespoon cornstarch
2 tablespoons vegetable oil
6 medium zucchini, thinly sliced
Steamed rice

In a small bowl, blend stock, oyster sauce, and cornstarch. Reserve.

Heat oil in a wok over medium heat; add zucchini and stir-fry 5 minutes, or until tender. Add sauce to zucchini and continue cooking, stirring constantly, until sauce is slightly thickened and zucchini is coated. Serve over rice. *Makes 3 cups zucchini.*

ORIENTAL VEGETABLES WITH BEEF SAUCE

1 cup ground beef
1 cup Basic Dog Broth (page 83)
1 teaspoon cornstarch mixed with 2 tablespoons soy sauce
3 tablespoons vegetable oil
1 clove garlic, minced
2 carrots, cut into ½-inch chunks
2 cups bok choy or Napa cabbage, cut into 1-inch pieces
1 cup snow peas, trimmed and strings removed
3 scallions, finely chopped
Steamed rice or kibble (pages 73–80)

Place beef in a cold skillet and cook over medium heat, breaking up meat with a wooden spoon until crumbly. Add broth and soy sauce mixture; cook until gravy is very slightly thickened. Reserve.

Heat oil in a wok over medium-high heat; add garlic and brown lightly. Add carrots and stir-fry 4 minutes. Add bok choy and stir-fry 4 minutes. Add meat sauce, snow peas, and scallions; cook 2 minutes, coating vegetables thoroughly with sauce. Serve over rice or kibble. *Makes 5 cups vegetables.*

This dish, chock-full of protein and fiber and abundant in vitamins A and C, is perfect for the Shar-Pei, the Chinese fighting dog that has become enormously popular among upwardly mobile urbanites. The dog's oversized, wrinkled skin was probably advantageous during the time it was bred for combat—the numerous folds prevented its adversary from getting a grip and injuring vital blood vessels. Today, however, the Shar-Pei is carefully bred as a benign—and expensive—pet.

STEAMED MIXED VEGETABLES WITH HERBED BUTTER SAUCE

Some dogs are very light eaters and prefer food that is plain and cleanly cooked. Others, who are sedentary, will benefit from an occasional vegetarian meal. These simple steamed vegetables with their piquant mustard sauce will provide a dish rich in carbohydrates and a wide range of vitamins.

4 tablespoons (½ stick) unsalted butter
1 tablespoon chopped fresh tarragon
1 tablespoon chopped Italian parsley
1 teaspoon dry mustard
1 teaspoon wine vinegar
Salt
Freshly ground black pepper
2 potatoes, cut into bite-size pieces
1 head cauliflower, divided into florets
2 carrots, cut into bite-size pieces
1 cup peas
1 onion, cut into 1-inch dice

Melt butter over low heat in a small saucepan. Add tarragon, parsley, mustard, vinegar, and salt and pepper to taste. Stir until mixture is heated, then let stand at least 15 minutes for flavors to blend.

Bring a large pot of water to a boil. Add potatoes, which will cook a total of 20 minutes. After 7 minutes add cauliflower; after another 7 minutes add carrots, and 5 to 6 minutes before end of cooking time add peas. When all vegetables are tender, drain and transfer to a towel. Reheat butter sauce and pour over vegetables. *Makes 5 to 6 cups vegetables.*

SAUCES

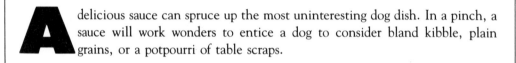

A delicious sauce can spruce up the most uninteresting dog dish. In a pinch, a sauce will work wonders to entice a dog to consider bland kibble, plain grains, or a potpourri of table scraps.

ROVER'S ROUX OR GOOD DOGGIE GRAVY

¼ cup pan drippings
¼ cup unbleached all-purpose flour
2 cups Basic Dog Broth (page 83) or 2 cups water mixed with 2 tablespoons beef bouillon
    powder
Pinch of salt (optional)

In the roasting pan or a saucepan, heat drippings over medium heat. Add flour slowly and cook until browned, stirring constantly. Slowly stir in broth or water and bouillon powder and cook, stirring, until gravy is thick. Add salt if broth was used. *Makes 2 cups gravy.*

Here's an excellent way to use up pan drippings from a roast or chops. The drippings might be too high in cholesterol for your family, but they won't go to waste if you make this thick gravy—just the thing to ladle over leftover meat and kibble.

Sauce Chiennaise

This is a particularly luxurious sauce, meant for special occasions and definitely not for the dieting dog. Rich in butter and eggs, it is best served over a low-calorie entree.

8 tablespoons (1 stick) unsalted butter
1 tablespoon minced shallot
¼ cup sherry vinegar
¼ teaspoon dried tarragon
Salt
2 egg yolks

In the top of a double boiler, melt butter over direct medium-low heat. Add shallot and sauté gently 2 to 3 minutes. Stir in vinegar, tarragon, and salt to taste; cook briefly until heated. Remove from heat and allow mixture to cool to barely warm.

When ready to serve, whisk egg yolks into sauce and place pan over simmering water. Cook sauce, whisking constantly, until thickened and creamy. *Makes about ⅔ cup sauce.*

RED ROVER VALLEY TEXAS-STYLE BARBECUE SAUCE

1 clove garlic, minced
1 medium onion, finely chopped
½ cup catsup
½ cup water
1 tablespoon molasses
1 tablespoon Worcestershire sauce
1 teaspoon Dijon mustard
Salt
Freshly ground black pepper

Combine all ingredients in a bowl. Use sauce to baste ribs, steaks, frankfurters, or hamburgers over a medium fire. *Makes about 1½ cups sauce.*

Not too hot, not too sweet, this recipe was contributed by a cattle-herding dog who found it to be just the right seasoning for snakes, lizards, armadillos, and other varmints.

PEANUT LOVER'S SAUCE

For some reason most dogs are crazy about peanut butter. In our house, the dogs beg for peanut butter, and it's hard to avoid their plaintive doggy stares while making a peanut butter sandwich destined for human consumption. This peanut-based sauce is based on a traditional Javanese sauce. Rich in protein, it can be used sparingly over salads, vegetables, breads, or kibble.

1 tablespoon peanut oil
½ cup chopped onion
1 cup peanut butter (smooth or chunky)
½ cup water
½ clove garlic, minced
1 tablespoon honey
1½ teaspoons tamari sauce
1½ teaspoons grated fresh ginger
Drop of hot pepper sauce
1½ cups milk

Heat oil in large saucepan over medium heat. Add onion and sauté until soft and transparent. Add peanut butter and water and mix slowly and well to form a paste. Stir in garlic, honey, tamari, ginger, and hot pepper sauce. Add milk slowly, stirring constantly until sauce is well blended. Heat sauce through, but do not bring to a boil. Serve warm or cold. *Makes almost 1 quart sauce.*

CHOP-LICKER'S LIVER SAUCE

3 tablespoons unsalted butter
1 cup chicken livers
1 cup Chicken Stock (page 84)
1 tablespoon cornstarch
2 teaspoons chopped chives
Salt

Melt 1 tablespoon butter in small skillet over medium-high heat. Add chicken livers and sauté until livers are cooked through, about 10 minutes. Transfer livers to food processor or blender and purée, adding enough stock to make a smooth emulsion.

Blend cornstarch and remaining stock. Heat remaining 2 tablespoons butter in a saucepan over medium heat. Stir in cornstarch mixture, chives, and salt to taste, and cook until sauce is smooth and thickened. Add puréed liver and mix well. Add water if necessary to thin sauce. Serve over kibbles or grains. *Makes about 2 cups sauce.*

"Chops" is a slang expression for lips. To "lick one's chops" indicates delight as delicious food is savored. Some pets carry their appreciation to an extreme: One of our cats holds the house record for chop licking, with over fifty licks for one piece of chicken! This liver sauce is guaranteed to create a frenzy of chop licking in your home.

Far East Dog Sauce

This sauce will lend an Oriental flavor to any dish. It is a versatile accompaniment to fish, poultry, or meat.

Infrequent Flyers
The International Air Transportation Association discourages some dogs from flying:

- nursing mothers and unweaned pups
- females in heat
- pups under eight weeks old
- short-nosed dogs with respiratory problems

British Airways does not accept any snub-nosed breeds, including pugs, Pekingese, bulldogs, and boxers.

1 clove garlic, minced
1 cup Chicken Stock (page 84)
2 tablespoons tamari sauce
2 tablespoons cornstarch
1 tablespoon dry sherry
1 teaspoon brown bean sauce (available in Oriental food stores)
1 teaspoon sugar
¼ teaspoon dry mustard

Place all ingredients in blender and run motor until all ingredients are well combined. Pour mixture into a small saucepan, bring to a boil over medium heat, and cook, stirring constantly, until sauce is thickened and slightly reduced. *Makes about 1 cup sauce.*

CANINE CURRY SAUCE

1 cup Chicken Stock (page 84)
1 tablespoon cornstarch dissolved in 2 tablespoons water
½ cup plain lowfat yogurt
½ teaspoon ground cumin
½ teaspoon ground coriander
½ teaspoon turmeric

In a small saucepan, combine stock and cornstarch mixture. Bring to a boil over medium heat and cook, stirring constantly, until thickened. Remove pan from heat; whisk in yogurt, cumin, coriander, and turmeric. *Makes 1⅓ cups sauce.*

Mild curry flavor and protein-rich yogurt give this sauce just enough zip to rekindle your dog's interest in kibble or other grain dishes. It's especially good served with rice and eggs (see Tail Wagger's Eggs with Saffron Rice, page 70) or over bulgur wheat.

What really goes on in their tiny minds?

As dogs became domesticated, their brain capacity was reduced until it was 20 to 30 percent less than that of a comparably sized wolf. Still, many people like to think their dogs are humans in fur coats. Dogs are intelligent to the extent that, when trained to the maximum of their capabilities, they can learn certain tasks and signals: how to associate specific commands with equally specific behavior and rewards. At their best, dogs can reach the approximate intelligence of a seven-year-old child. They're keenly aware of our nonverbal behavior and their doggy radar picks up our emotions—sometimes they even seem to know what we're going to do before we tell them.

Much of a dog's intelligence is instinctual, including the chase instinct (ask any squirrel) and the territorial instinct (ask any mailman). Dogs will revert to pack instincts if allowed, and for this reason it is best to keep a dog from roaming with the neighborhood gang. The maternal instinct is built into most female dogs.

DECADENT DOGGIE DESSERTS

Dogs love sweets, and unlike their human counterparts, they don't have to worry a lot about tooth decay. However, too much of a good thing can cause nutritional problems, so the recipes offered here are for occasional use, such as a dog birthday, holidays, and for other special doggie needs.

It's an old myth that sweets are the cause of worms. But it is true that too much sugar in the diet will ruin a dog's appetite for more nutritious food. An excess of sugar also tends to create a nutritional imbalance, since sugar requires many vitamins and nutrients to metabolize. For that reason these desserts are made with very little sugar—although not so little as to render them unappealing to your dog's sweet tooth—and with the most nutritious ingredients: vegetables, eggs, dairy foods, and grains.

Many dogs love fruit with a passion, so you may slowly introduce small amounts of fresh fruit in the diet: Bananas, pears, apples, grapes, and melons are all popular with dogs.

HASTY DOG PUDDING

2 cups milk
½ cup cornmeal
2 tablespoons molasses
2 tablespoons honey
2 large eggs, beaten
½ teaspoon salt
¼ teaspoon freshly grated nutmeg

Preheat oven to 350° F. and butter a 1-quart baking dish.

Bring milk to a boil in a medium saucepan over medium heat. Add cornmeal slowly, stirring constantly; cook over low heat until thickened. Stir in molasses and honey, then beat in eggs, salt, and nutmeg. Pour mixture into prepared baking dish and bake 1 hour. Serve warm or at room temperature. *Makes about 2¾ cups pudding.*

The fastest time recorded for racing greyhounds is just over 41 miles an hour. Dogs who exercise hard have increased caloric requirements which can be met by the addition of a simple dog dessert in the meal plan.

MILLET SURPRISE

Often a convalescing dog will need a special boost to keep its appetite up. This dessert combines a nutritious grain with a light, sweet sauce that your dog will joyfully lap up.

1 cup millet
3 cups water
½ teaspoon salt
½ cup maple syrup
1 teaspoon cinnamon
½ teaspoon ground cloves

Preheat oven to 350° F. and butter a 1-quart baking dish.

Place millet, water, and salt in a saucepan and bring to a boil. Remove from heat and stir in maple syrup, cinnamon, and cloves. Pour mixture into prepared baking dish and bake 45 minutes. Serve warm or at room temperature. *Makes about 1 quart pudding.*

YAM PUDDING

2 cups finely grated raw yams
3 large eggs, separated
2 cups milk
½ cup honey
½ cup light corn syrup
3 tablespoons unsalted butter, melted
½ teaspoon cinnamon
¼ teaspoon ground cloves
¼ teaspoon freshly grated nutmeg

Preheat oven to 350° F. and butter a 2-quart baking dish.

In a mixing bowl, combine yams, egg yolks, milk, honey, corn syrup, butter, cinnamon, cloves, and nutmeg; beat until well mixed. In another bowl, beat egg whites until stiff. Stir a large spoonful of whites into yam mixture, then fold in remaining whites.

Turn mixture into prepared baking dish and bake 1 hour, or until firm. *Makes about 1 quart pudding.*

Most Southern dogs know how good naturally sweet yams are. Nothing could be better than a dreamy dog nap on a satisfied dog tummy filled with a splendid meal that includes this delicious pudding.

If your dog has problems with incontinence, a cedar chip bed is not for him. The combination of urine and cedar chips can promote bacterial infections.

TOFU WITH HONEY SAUCE

Soy products are very high in protein and are often included in commercial pet food. Tofu is extremely digestible, and its blandness is soothing for a dog with an upset stomach. Dogs are crazy about these honey-coated morsels—they'll perform all sorts of tricks to get their fill.

1 package (16 ounces) firm tofu
2 tablespoons cornstarch
2½ tablespoons sesame seeds
2 cups vegetable oil for deep frying
½ cup honey

Rinse and drain tofu, then cut into 1-inch squares. On a plate or piece of wax paper, mix together cornstarch and 2 tablespoons sesame seeds. Roll tofu in sesame mixture.

In a wok, heat oil over high heat until hot but not smoking. Fry tofu a few pieces at a time, turning once, until golden brown. Drain on paper towels.

In a small saucepan, heat honey and enough water to make a light sauce. Place tofu on plate and pour sauce over it, garnishing with a sprinkling of sesame seeds. *Makes 2 cups tofu dessert.*

PUMPKIN IN SYRUP

1 medium pumpkin
⅓ cup honey
⅓ cup raisins

Preheat oven to 350° F. Pour 1 inch of water into a large shallow baking pan.

Cut open pumpkin, discarding stem, and scrape out seeds and slimy membranes. (Don't peel the skin—it's a good source of roughage for your dog.) Cut pumpkin into 2-inch pieces and place in prepared baking pan. Bake 1 hour, or until pumpkin is tender.

In a small saucepan, heat honey and enough water to make a light syrup. Add raisins and simmer sauce 10 minutes. Transfer pumpkin to a shallow bowl and pour sauce over it. *Makes about 1 quart of pumpkin and syrup.*

This is an excellent recipe to use up some of the extra pumpkins usually so abundant at harvest time. At Halloween, your dog can't carve his own pumpkin, so the next best thing is to feed him one.

SWEET POTATO PIE

3 large cooked sweet potatoes
2 large eggs, separated
½ cup maple syrup
1 teaspoon salt
½ teaspoon ground allspice
¼ teaspoon ground ginger
¼ teaspoon ground cloves
1 unbaked 9-inch pie crust

Preheat oven to 350° F.

Peel sweet potatoes and mash in a mixing bowl. Beat in egg yolks, maple syrup, salt, allspice, ginger, and cloves. In another bowl, beat egg whites until stiff. Stir a spoonful of whites into sweet potato mixture, then fold in remaining whites.

Turn filling into pie crust and bake 30 to 40 minutes, or until filling is just set. Serve at room temperature. *Makes one 9-inch pie.*

This dessert will delight your dog's sweet tooth and also provide essential proteins.

Chocolate is a food that is harmful to dogs although of course most of them like it and will eat it in such baked goods as brownies or in confections such as chocolate bars. A chocoholic dog will usually have severe diarrhea and can actually be poisoned by chocolate.

FOOD FOR SPECIAL NEEDS

DIET DISHES

Cold Carnivore Salad, Cabbage Rolls, Vegetable Pie with Potato Crust—these are recipes that will boost the morale of any dog on a diet. Rich in flavor and texture but low in calories, this is food that will help you to help your dog reduce successfully. Be sure to use the chart at the end of this chapter to record your dog's progress. It doesn't occur to most of us to serve salads to our dogs, but most of them will eagerly consume fresh vegetables that are accompanied by a savory dressing.

Old Mother Hubbard
Went to the cupboard
To fetch her poor dog a bone
When she got there
The cupboard was bare
And so the poor dog had none.

COLD CARNIVORE SALAD

1 cup olive oil
1 teaspoon minced garlic
1 teaspoon Dijon mustard
1 egg yolk
¼ cup balsamic vinegar
Salt
½ head cabbage, shredded
1 cup diced cooked beef
4 cooked small new potatoes, cut into halves
¼ cup chopped Italian parsley

To prepare dressing, in a bowl whisk together oil, garlic, mustard, egg yolk, vinegar, and salt to taste until mixture is emulsified. Set aside.

Spread cabbage on plate and arrange beef and potatoes over it. Pour dressing sparingly over salad, sprinkle with parsley, and serve. *Makes 1½ quarts salad.*

The bond with a true dog is as lasting as the ties of this earth can ever be, a fact which should be noted by anyone who decides to acquire a canine friend.
—Konrad Lorenz,
Man Meets Dog

Dogs have an amazing ability to find their way home over long distances after becoming lost. More than one dog has come to a city it has never been in before and been able to find its owners' new home.

Mediterranean Salad

Bulgur wheat is higher in protein than brown rice, chicken wings, or tofu! And since most dogs dote on raisins, this recipe will be a special treat.

2 cups bulgur
Salt
2 cups water
¼ cup Basic Dog Broth (page 83)
1 tablespoon olive oil
½ cup chopped walnuts
¼ cup raisins
2 tablespoons chopped Italian parsley
Freshly ground black pepper
1 head lettuce, torn into bite-size pieces

Combine bulgur, salt to taste, and water in a saucepan; bring to a boil over medium heat. Reduce heat and simmer, covered, about 15 minutes, then remove cover and let grain cool to room temperature.

Add walnuts, raisins, parsley, and salt and pepper to taste to the bulgur and toss gently. Combine broth and oil in a small bowl; add to bulgur mixture and toss again.

Make a bed of lettuce in dog dish. Spoon bulgur on lettuce and serve at room temperature. *Makes about 1 quart salad.*

Diet Salad with Hamburger Dressing

½ cup ground beef
1 cup Basic Dog Broth (page 83)
1 tablespoon olive oil
Salt
Freshly ground black pepper
1 cup bite-size pieces lettuce
1 tablespoon miller's bran
½ cup 1% fat cottage cheese

Place beef in a cold skillet and cook over medium heat, breaking up meat with a wooden spoon until crumbly. Drain beef on paper towels, then transfer to a small bowl and add broth, oil, and salt and pepper to taste.

   Distribute lettuce pieces in dog's dish, pour beef dressing over lettuce, and sprinkle bran on top. Scoop cottage cheese into center of salad and serve. *Makes 2 cups salad.*

The Dogs eat of the crumbs which fall from their masters' table.
—Matthew 15:27

The cocker spaniel is one breed that should be very careful of gaining extra weight. Take Freckles, for example, an affable cocker residing at the Kalorama Guest House in Washington, D.C. A regular fixture on the sunny breakfast porch, Freckles begs a bit of scone from one guest, a crumb of croissant from another, a morsel of muffin from a third, day in and day out. For Freckles, this amounts to hundreds of unneeded calories a day—an occupational hazard that keeps her owner ever vigilant about Freckles's weight.

SLIMMING TUNA SLAW

According to the *Guinness Book of World Records*, one of the largest dogs on record was Schwarzwald Hof Duke, a St. Bernard who tipped the scales at 295 pounds—and lived to be only 5 years old. This wonderful, crunchy salad will help trim a few pounds off any overweight pooch. The amount of raw onion can be reduced, or eliminate it altogether if your dog won't eat it.

1 head cabbage, shredded
1 carrot, grated
¼ cup finely chopped onion
½ cup olive oil
¼ cup red wine vinegar
1 tablespoon Dijon mustard
1 teaspoon sugar
1 can (6½ ounces) water-packed tuna

In a large bowl, toss together cabbage, carrot, and onion. In a small bowl, whisk together oil, vinegar, mustard, and sugar. Drain tuna, flake it into dressing, and mix well. Pour tuna dressing over vegetables and toss until well mixed. Serve at room temperature. *Makes 1 quart salad.*

CABBAGE ROLLS

10 large cabbage leaves
1 cup shredded cooked chicken
1 cup cooked rice
1 teaspoon chopped Italian parsley
½ teaspoon dried oregano
Salt
Freshly ground black pepper
½ cup plain lowfat yogurt
½ to 1 cup Chicken Stock (page 84)
½ cup grated Cheddar cheese

Preheat oven to 350° F. Oil a baking dish large enough to accommodate 10 cabbage rolls in one layer.

With a sharp paring knife, trim away the thick white vein at the base of cabbage leaves. Bring a large pot of water to a boil, add cabbage leaves, and simmer until tender enough to roll. Transfer leaves to paper towels and allow to cool.

In a mixing bowl, combine chicken, rice, parsley, oregano, and salt and pepper to taste. Add enough yogurt to bind the mixture and produce a creamy consistency.

Spread out cabbage leaves and place 2 tablespoons chicken mixture in center of each leaf. Roll up leaves, tucking in sides, and arrange cabbage rolls in baking dish. Pour in enough stock to reach 1 inch up sides of dish, then sprinkle with cheese. Cover and bake 30 minutes. Serve warm. *Makes 10 cabbage rolls.*

Cabbage is rich in vitamin C and provides roughage for the dieting dog. The well-balanced filling here is a meal in itself. For smaller dogs, freeze special portions to serve with soup at another time.

Stress
Our pets identify with us, and they are subject to the influence of our emotional states. A dog's personality is affected by its master's attitude. An owner who is bored, depressed, angry, inconsistent, indifferent, tense, or very harsh or permissive contributes to the pet's behavior.

VEGETABLE PIE WITH POTATO CRUST

This nutritious dish can be assembled from any vegetables you have on hand—all that's necessary is a good assortment.

Crust

4 medium unpeeled potatoes, cut into chunks
2 tablespoons margarine
Salt
Freshly ground black pepper
1 egg yolk, beaten

Filling

2½ cups mixed vegetables, or ½ cup cubed carrots, ½ cup cubed peeled broccoli stems, ½
    cup cubed zucchini, ½ cup green beans cut into ½-inch lengths, and ½ cup corn
    kernels
¼ teaspoon dried oregano
¼ teaspoon dried thyme
Salt
Freshly ground black pepper
2 tablespoons cornstarch
1 cup Chicken Stock (page 84)
¼ cup sherry

Preheat oven to 400° F. and grease a 9-inch pie pan.

    To make crust, place potatoes in a saucepan with water to cover, bring to a boil, uncovered, 15 to 20 minutes, or until tender. Drain and mash potatoes, adding margarine and salt and pepper to taste. Spread mashed potatoes evenly over bottom and up sides of pie pan. Bake 35 to 40 minutes, brushing crust with egg yolk after 15 minutes. When crust is firm and golden brown, remove from oven and cool.

Reduce oven temperature to 350° F.

To make filling, place carrots, broccoli, and green beans in steamer basket and steam, covered, over boiling water 7 to 8 minutes, or until tender. Add zucchini during last 4 minutes of cooking. Transfer cooked vegetables to a mixing bowl. Add corn, oregano, thyme, and salt and pepper to taste, and toss well to mix. Turn vegetable mixture into cooled pie crust.

Put cornstarch into a small bowl; stir in stock, then sherry. Pour this mixture over vegetables and bake pie 25 minutes, or until very hot and sauce has thickened. *Makes one 9-inch pie.*

Collar Common Sense

Allow your dog to wear only one collar at a time. A choke chain, used for obedience training, should not be worn with any other collar and must be attached properly so that the chain hangs free when not in use. To do this, be sure the loose end is threaded through the opposite end over the top of the dog's neck. This way the collar will always be in a relaxed position. The collar should fit properly, with a three- to four-inch slack.

If you buy a dog collar that is not adjustable, be sure it is not too tight. You should be able to slide two or three fingers underneath it.

TOFU EGG DROP SOUP

Tofu is an exceptionally good source of protein, supplying only slightly fewer grams per pound than chicken wings and backs. It's bland and easily digestible. As a filler in your dog's diet, tofu is a palatable meat substitute or extender. In this soup, the tofu takes on the flavor of the rich chicken stock.

6 cups Chicken Stock (page 84)
1 package (16 ounces) firm tofu, drained, rinsed, and cut into 1-inch cubes
2 scallions, chopped
2 tablespoons chopped Italian parsley
2 tablespoons tamari sauce
2 tablespoons cornstarch dissolved in 3 tablespoons cold water
1 egg, beaten

In a saucepan, bring stock to a boil; add tofu and reduce heat. Add scallions, parsley, tamari, and cornstarch mixture. Return soup to a boil, stir in egg, and let boil just for a moment. *Makes about 2 quarts soup.*

SLENDERIZING SAVORY TRIPE SOUP

1 pound tripe
1 teaspoon salt
½ lemon, sliced
6 cups water
1 carrot, chopped
2 turnips, chopped
2 scallions, thinly sliced
1 clove garlic, minced
¼ cup sherry
2 tablespoons tamari sauce
2 peppercorns
1 small head cabbage, shredded

The key to using tripe successfully is in the precooking, which helps tenderize the meat. Be sure to purchase the freshest tripe possible—you may need to special order it from your butcher. Either honeycomb or smooth tripe will work very well in this recipe, although honeycomb is the tenderer of the two.

To precook tripe, cut into bite-size pieces and place in a saucepan with cold water to cover by 2 to 3 inches. Add salt and lemon slices; bring to a boil over high heat, then cook 3 to 4 minutes. Drain tripe; repeat process twice. During last cooking, reduce heat and simmer tripe, covered, until it is tender enough to be pierced with a fork.

Drain tripe and place in a soup kettle. Add 6 cups water and bring to a boil over high heat. Lower heat and simmer tripe again, covered, 1 hour more.

Remove meat with slotted spoon and reserve. Add carrots and turnips to broth, bring to a boil, and cook about 5 minutes, or until tender. Add tripe, scallions, garlic, sherry, tamari, and peppercorns; simmer 15 minutes to blend flavors. Add cabbage and cook 15 minutes longer. Serve warm. *Makes 2½ quarts soup.*

DOG DAYS WILTED SALAD

The "dog days" of June through August received their name in ancient Egypt, when Sirius, the Dog Star, was visible for a forty-day period marked by stifling humidity and heat. The star itself was believed at that time to increase the sun's heat, thus contributing to the sweltering temperatures, and dogs, so the superstition went, were susceptible to demonic possession, madness, and rabies during this period.

Mad dogs and Englishmen go out in the midday sun.
—Noel Coward

2 tablespoons olive oil
1 clove garlic, minced
1 head Iceberg lettuce, cut into chunks
2 cups cooked fresh or frozen peas, snow peas, or chopped broccoli
1 cup bite-size pieces cooked lean meat or fish
1 beef bouillon cube dissolved in 1 cup hot water
¼ teaspoon dried thyme

Heat oil in a skillet over medium heat; add garlic and brown. Add lettuce and stir-fry until limp. Add peas, meat, or fish bouillon mixture, and thyme; raise heat and bring to a boil. Cook just until all ingredients are heated through. Serve warm or cold, alone or over steamed rice or kibble. *Makes 1 quart salad.*

Dog Weight Chart

Name of Dog _____

Ideal Weight _____

Date	Weight	Daily Intake	Notes

SKIN TREATMENT

Your dog's skin is a barometer of its health and resistance to disease and stress. Healthy skin and coat reflect a healthy and well-cared-for dog. But for some dogs, a lush, glossy coat is only a dream. According to veterinarians, skin problems rank number one among their clientele. Dogs can suffer intensely from itchy, dry, flaky skin; greasy, dull, matted coats; bad odors; rashes; "hot spots"; and hair loss. Nothing is more discouraging than to see your pet constantly scratching, biting, and otherwise ravaging its coat and skin, all of which aggravate the underlying problem.

Since all dogs continually harbor skin disease bacteria, it is important to pay special attention to the skin and coat so that a skin irritation doesn't become serious or chronic. The skin is the largest organ of the dog's body, and it will reflect hormone imbalances, poor nutrition, stress, allergies, and parasite infestation. Heredity plays a role in skin sensitivity and unfortunately some breeds have more sensitive skin than others. Among the breeds that need additional preventive maintenance are golden retrievers, dobermans, dachshunds, Irish setters, poodles, beagles, fox terriers, and Scottish terriers.

Preventive care goes a long way in dealing with coat and skin problems—both from the inside and on the outside. There is much that can be done to keep the coat in top condition. If your dog has any skin problems, here's what you can do immediately:

- Do not feed your dog any foods containing additives or impurities.
- Give a balanced dietary vitamin supplement (Pet Tabs plus Zinc) for vitamins A, B, C, and E, and add brewer's yeast to your pet's food.
- For dry skin, add extra corn or safflower oil to the diet to provide essential fatty acids, and small amounts of cod liver oil for the coat.
- Keep dog out of sun. If your dog spends a lot of time poolside, use a sun block on its nose, especially if the nose is pink or very light-colored.
- Don't allow the dog to sleep next to radiators in the winter.
- If dog has walked on salted surfaces during the winter, wash off paws immediately and rub petroleum jelly (Vaseline) on them for protection.
- Wash coat with fresh water after dog has been swimming in marshy, polluted, or stagnant water.
- Get rid of fleas.

Cleanliness is essential for the health of your dog's

skin and coat. Daily grooming keeps the dog looking its best and also gives you a chance to inspect for parasites, burrs, mats, or any skin irregularities. Long-haired breeds needs brushing and grooming to bring oil to the ends of the hair.

One last thing: Most dogs rarely need a bath. Too much bathing aggravates some coat conditions and increases dry coat and flaky skin. The correct shampoo is essential when you do bathe the dog. Shampoo made just for dogs is best. For hypersensitive skin, purchase specially formulated dog shampoo from your veterinarian.

Summer skin problems

- fleas, ticks, mosquitos, sunburn, grass pollen allergies

Winter skin problems

- dry heat, chemically treated sidewalks, severe temperature changes

Here's the full doggie spa routine:

- a luxurious bath with special dog soap
- an elbow and paw-pad rub with lanolin
- a comb-out with a lanolin spray

Bathing Tips

- Because the dog will usually not shake itself until its head or ears are wet, start washing your dog at the rear and work your way forward to prevent yourself from getting soaked during the washing process
- rinse the dog's entire body before you wash the head
- when washing the head, be careful not to get shampoo in your dog's eyes, and use a washcloth to wash the face
- cover the entire dog with a towel (or towels) immediately after rinsing the head to minimize the dog-shower effects as the pooch instinctively shakes itself to dry off

GOLDEN SKIN ELIXIR

This recipe can be used as long as needed to perk up a dull, dry coat. Just pour it over the dog's food, and in no time at all your dog's coat will be restored to a glowing, healthy condition.

1 cup Chicken Stock (page 84)
1 hard-cooked egg, with shell
⅓ cup wheat germ
1 tablespoon brewer's yeast
½ clove garlic, crushed
2 tablespoons corn oil

Place stock, egg and shell, wheat germ, brewer's yeast, garlic, and oil in a blender or food processor and purée. Pour over dog's food. *Makes about 1½ cups elixir.*

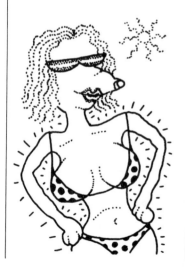

FOOD FOR YOUR AGING DOG

Keeping pace with the changing nutritional needs of the aging dog requires an understanding of the dog's physical changes. One of the main problems of the aging dog is that the sense of smell begins to wane, so it's more difficult to interest your dog in food. On the other hand, because a dog slows down as it grows older, less food will be needed to maintain good health.

As some of your dog's organs age, their functions may be affected; this will determine what kinds of foods that are easy to digest, lower in total protein than during his vigorous years, and lower in salt.

Most aging dogs have an increased need for fluids as their kidneys slow down, so soups are an excellent choice, especially since the heady aroma of a simmering soup will arouse that flagging sense of smell.

To maintain your dog's weight, it's often necessary to increase the fat intake since food isn't absorbed as efficiently as before. The geriatric dog will also benefit from vitamin supplementation. My sixteen-year-old Emily improved her mobility, regained bladder control, and was no longer plagued with bladder infections after her diet was supplemented with a large daily dose of vitamin C. The change was dramatic and swift, and she was grateful to be able to climb steps easily and to have control over her bladder for a much longer period.

Some oldsters become downright peculiar and faddish about their food, so, at their stage in life, why not humor them. Let your dog have an occasional croissant, if that's his pleasure; part with that last morsel of truffled foie gras or lobster bordelaise.

SILVER SNOUT STEW

This rich dish, which includes liver for high-quality protein and a mélange of vegetables for fiber and complex carbohydrates, is best seasoned lightly with tamari and just a touch of sherry. Soak pieces of bread in the broth for a delicious feast.

1 pound chicken gizzards
2 tablespoons unsalted butter
4 potatoes, cut into ½-inch pieces
2 onions, chopped
2 carrots, chopped
1 stalk celery, thinly sliced
1 tablespoon dried oregano
Salt
Freshly ground pepper
1 large can (46 ounces) chicken broth or 6 cups Chicken Stock (page 84)
½ cup whole-grain or Scotch barley
2 tablespoons tamari sauce
2 tablespoons dry sherry
Bread cut into 1-inch squares

Place gizzards in saucepan, cover with water, and bring to a boil over high heat. Reduce heat and simmer gizzards, uncovered, 45 minutes, adding water as necessary. Drain gizzards, reserving troth, and cut into bite-size pieces.

Place gizzards and reserved cooking liquid, chicken broth, and barley in a soup kettle; bring to a boil. Reduce heat and simmer soup, covered, 30 minutes, or until barley is tender.

Meanwhile, melt butter in a large skillet over medium heat. Add potatoes, onions, carrots, and celery and sauté until vegetables are coated with butter and somewhat softened. As vegetables cook, add oregano and salt and pepper to taste.

Add vegetables to soup; stir in tamari and sherry and cook 15 minutes longer. Place bread pieces in dog's bowl and ladle broth and vegetables over them. *Makes 3 quarts soup.*

GRAY PANTHER PASTA

1 pound pasta
2 tablespoons unsalted butter
2 tablespoons all-purpose flour
1½ cups milk
1 cup freshly grated Romano cheese
Salt
¼ teaspoon freshly ground white pepper
2 cups diced cooked boneless chicken

Pasta is an excellent food for the aging dog. It's versatile as well; you can add chicken, beef, or sausage to it. If your dog needs extra calories, make a rich and buttery cream sauce. Hot or cold, pasta is a favorite of dogs of all ages. The shape is immaterial to your dog, but you'll find the food stays in the bowl if you serve short noodles instead of the traditional long spaghetti.

Cook pasta according to package instructions, then rinse and drain. Reserve pasta in large mixing bowl.

In a small saucepan, melt butter over medium-low heat. Stir in flower and whisk until it begins to turn golden. Over medium heat, add milk gradually, stirring constantly; cook until sauce is thickened. Add cheese, salt to taste, and pepper.

Add chicken to pasta, pour in sauce, and toss to mix well. Serve warm. Leftovers can be reheated in top of double boiler or in microwave. *Makes 3 quarts pasta and sauce.*

NOODLE CASSEROLE À LA METHUSELAH

The oldest dog logged in the *Guinness Book of World Records* was Bluey, a Queensland, Australia, dog who lived for twenty-nine years and five months. Translated into human years, that's probably close to 150 years of age. Vigorous for many years, Bluey worked as an active sheep and cattle dog for over two decades.

4 tablespoons (½ stick) unsalted butter
1 pound lean boneless turkey, cut into bite-size pieces
1 pound egg noodles
2 cups milk
1 cup Chicken Stock (page 84)
½ cup grated mild Cheddar cheese
2 tablespoons chopped Italian parsley
1 cup dried bread crumbs
2 hard-cooked eggs, coarsely chopped

Preheat oven to 350° F. and grease a 13 × 9-inch oblong baking dish.

Melt 2 tablespoons butter over medium heat in a skillet. Add turkey and sauté until lightly browned and cooked through. Reserve.

Cook noodles according to package instructions. Drain and place in large mixing bowl.

In a small saucepan, heat milk and stock over medium heat. Add cheese and cook until cheese is melted, stirring constantly. In a small skillet, melt remaining 2 tablespoons butter over medium heat; add bread crumbs and toss to combine.

Add turkey and cheese sauce to noodles and toss to mix well. Transfer mixture to prepared baking dish and sprinkle with hard-cooked eggs and bread crumbs. Bake 45 minutes, or until browned and bubbly. *Makes 3 quarts noodle casserole.*

EMILY'S ECCENTRIC PUDDING

4 tablespoons (½ stick) unsalted butter, melted
¼ cup sugar
2 large eggs, separated
8 ounces cottage cheese
2 cups milk
1 teaspoon vanilla extract
½ loaf sliced white bread (about 10 slices)
Raisins
Freshly grated nutmeg

In a mixing bowl, combine butter, sugar, egg whites, cottage cheese, ½ cup milk, and vanilla; stir well with a wooden spoon. The mixture will be thick.

Cut each slice of bread in half, place pieces in a single layer in a shallow dish, and pour remaining 1½ cups milk over them. Allow bread to soak until saturated, about 5 minutes.

Preheat oven to 350° F. and butter a 13 × 9-inch baking dish.

Remove bread from milk, reserving milk, and layer pieces in baking dish alternately with cottage cheese mixture, sprinkling each layer of cottage cheese with a few raisins.

Beat egg yolks. Add milk reserved from soaking bread and combine well. Pour mixture over bread and cheese, dust with nutmeg, and bake 30 to 40 minutes. Serve warm. *Makes 2 quarts pudding.*

A favorite of Emily's, this dish is high in carbohydrates and appeals to the sweet tooth in geriatric dogs.

Providential Pets

Pets have been found to have a therapeutic effect in nursing homes, prison programs, and psychiatric settings. Research shows that pets do influence their owners' health in positive, measurable ways.

A study on heart disease published in 1980 found that people who owned pets lived longer than those who didn't. Holding a pet can calm a person suffering from hypertension and help lower high blood pressure.

HEART SAVERS

A dog's heart can be affected by a number of disorders, including murmurs, congenital defects, and heartworm infestation. Some breeds are more prone to heart disease than others. Short-nosed breeds, such as the boxer, English bulldog, and Pekingese, often develop enlarged hearts due to the strain on their respiratory systems. The Chihuahua and the great Dane both experience heart valve problems. Other breeds with their share of cardiac illness include the beagle, poodle, fox terrier, Irish setter, German shepherd, German short-haired pointer, King Charles spaniel, and the Shetland sheepdog.

Five Ways to Keep Your Pet's Heart Healthy

- good nutrition
- prevention of overweight
- moderate, regular exercise
- prevention of heartworm and regular testing for it
- proper administration of medicine when prescribed

Nutrition for Heart-Sick Dogs

- no salt
- no preservatives
- no bacon or highly salted, processed meats
- high-quality protein

Heart-Saving Protein

Poultry: chicken, chicken gizzards, heart, and liver, turkey breast

Meat: beef heart, liver

Fish: water-packed tuna, carp, red snapper, halibut

BROILED HALIBUT

2 pounds boneless halibut steaks
¼ cup olive oil
Juice of 1 lemon
1 cup fresh or canned, salt-free tomato purée
2 tablespoons chopped fresh coriander (cilantro)
Steamed rice

Preheat broiler. Wash fish and inspect for and remove any bones. Place fish on broiler rack, baste with olive oil and lemon juice, and broil until cooked, turning and basting fish once and allowing 10 minutes per inch of thickness.

While fish is cooking, warm tomato purée in a small saucepan over low heat. Transfer halibut to dog dish, pour sauce over it, and dust top with coriander. *Makes about 1 quart fish and sauce.*

If your budget permits halibut steaks, your dog will experience canine ecstasy as he consumes this dish delicately seasoned with cilantro.

Poached Squid Soup

Squid delivers more protein per pound than choice beef chuck roast. Delicate in taste, this light soup will satisfy your dog's occasional craving for fish without subjecting him to the potential danger of tiny fish bones.

2 pounds squid
1 quart fish stock
2 scallions, chopped
2 tablespoons unsalted butter or margarine
1 tablespoon tamari sauce
Rice Balls (page 195)

Clean squid, or ask your fishmonger to do so when you purchase it; reserve tentacles. Wash squid well and cut into ½-inch slices.

In a soup kettle or large saucepan, bring stock to a boil; toss in squid and simmer 25 minutes. Add scallions, butter, and tamari, stirring until butter is melted. Serve in a bowl with Rice Balls. *Makes about 2 quarts soup.*

RICE BALLS

1 cup uncooked short-grained sushi or arborio rice (or use long-grain white rice)
2 cups water
Sesame seeds

In a saucepan, bring rice and water to a boil. Reduce heat and cook rice, covered, until tender and quite sticky. Remove cover and let cool.

When rice is cool enough to handle, wet your hands and form rice balls 1½ inches in diameter. Spread sesame seeds on a piece of wax paper and roll rice balls in them. *Makes about a dozen rice balls.*

Rice Balls provide the perfect solution for the fastidious eater who doesn't like to get his muzzle messy when munching up a plate of loose grains. The tiny balls can also be used as training treats.

TOFU-LIVER LOAF

The soy and liver team up to produce an abundance of high-quality, low-calorie, low-salt protein.

According to an ancient legend, during the creation of the world a giant chasm split the center of the earth: On one side there the animals and on the other side was man. The dog, alarmed at the growing distance between man and the animals, made a giant leap across the gap. He succeeded in bridging the gap, but clung tenuously to the edge with only his front paws. Man bent down and rescued the dog from the abyss and, since that day, dogs have been at man's side, a faithful and devoted friend, separate from all the other animals.

1 package (16 ounces) firm tofu
1 cup cooked rice
1 cup cooked calf's liver, finely chopped
1 cup dry bread crumbs
1 large egg
2 onions, finely chopped
2 tablespoons tamari sauce
¼ teaspoon chopped fresh thyme
¼ teaspoon chopped fresh sage
2 tablespoon unsalted butter or margarine, melted

The night before, freeze tofu, which will improve texture. The next day, defrost tofu at room temperature.

Preheat oven to 350° F. and grease a large loaf pan.

Rinse and drain tofu, blot with paper towels, and crumble into a mixing bowl. Add rice, liver, bread crumbs, egg, onions, tamari, thyme, and sage; mix well, adding water to moisten if mixture is too dry. Transfer mixture to loaf pan and bake 45 minutes. Serve warm. *Makes 1 loaf.*

BRAISED LIVER

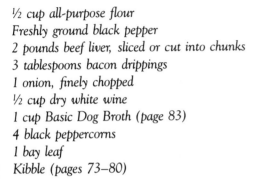

½ cup all-purpose flour
Freshly ground black pepper
2 pounds beef liver, sliced or cut into chunks
3 tablespoons bacon drippings
1 onion, finely chopped
½ cup dry white wine
1 cup Basic Dog Broth (page 83)
4 black peppercorns
1 bay leaf
Kibble (pages 73–80)

Combine flour with pepper to taste. Dredge liver in it, coating meat well on all sides.

In a Dutch oven, melt bacon drippings over moderately high heat; add liver, brown well on all sides. Add onion, wine, broth, peppercorns, and bay leaf; cover pan and bring to a simmer. Simmer, covered, 1 hour, or until tender.

Cut liver into bite-size pieces and serve over kibble with sauce. *Makes about 1 quart liver.*

An excellent recipe for dogs who need to build up their blood—but because it's rich in bacon fat, it's not for obese doggies.

KIDNEY DIETS

Kidney disease is one of the main killers of dogs. If you suspect that your dog may have a kidney disorder, you must take the dog to the veterinarian for diagnosis.

Some signs of kidney disease

- bad breath
- inability to pass urine
- excessive amounts of urine
- weight loss
- excessive thirst
- ulcers in the mouth
- muscle atrophy
- vomiting

Dogs with kidney dysfunction must undergo immediate dietary changes. If the problem isn't too severe, a reduction in protein will ease the burden on the damaged kidney. For more serious problems, a high-quality protein supplement is necessary; otherwise the animal will draw upon its own muscle stores to get the nutrients it needs and will quickly become emaciated. Most dogs, as they age, will benefit from a higher proportion of carbohydrate in the diet.

It's important to provide plenty of drinking water to help flush out the kidneys. Soups and stews, with their high liquid content, are good for the dog with a damaged kidney.

Here are some basic guidelines to help formulate the nutrients in a diet meant to benefit your dog's overtaxed kidneys:

- For mild disease, use one-third meat to two-thirds carbohydrates (volume measurements).
- For more severe disease, use one-quarter high-quality protein to three-quarters carbohydrates.
- There are excellent prescription diets, such as Hill's, which are available through a veterinarian, but they are expensive. Since the primary ingredients are chicken and rice, you will find that a home-cooked diet is much fresher and more economical.

KIDNEY SAVER'S PIE

1 tablespoon corn oil
1 cup broccoli florets, coarsely chopped
1 tablespoon fresh oregano leaves
1 teaspoon fresh thyme leaves
1 teaspoon chopped Italian parsley
2 cups cooked rice
½ cup cooked ground beef
1 hard-cooked egg, coarsely chopped
1 unbaked 9-inch pie shell
2 tablespoons cornstarch
1 cup Chicken Stock (page 84)

Preheat oven to 400° F.

Heat oil in a small skillet over moderate heat. Add broccoli, oregano, thyme, and parsley; sauté 4 or 5 minutes, until broccoli is just cooked. Transfer broccoli to a mixing bowl. Add rice, beef, and egg and mix well. Scrape mixture into pie shell.

In a small bowl, dissolve cornstarch with a little stock, then add remaining stock to bowl. Pour mixture over filling and bake pie 30 minutes. Let cool before serving. *Makes one 9-inch pie.*

This is a tasty, well-seasoned dish that your dog will find delicious despite its low meat content.

Marvelous Mexican Bean and Beef Stew

The rice, beans, and tortillas make this dish rich in complex carbohydrates. As a bonus, the beans are a fine source of potassium, necessary for the optimum functioning of your pet's nervous system.

1 cup uncooked brown rice
2½ cups water
1 tablespoon corn oil
1 cup ground beef
1 onion, chopped
1 green bell pepper, chopped
1 stalk celery, chopped
1 cup cooked pink beans
1 cup Basic Dog Broth (page 83)
2 tablespoons chopped Italian parsley
½ teaspoon chopped fresh coriander (cilantro)
1 teaspoon chili powder
½ teaspoon ground cumin
½ cup corn kernels
Steamed flour tortillas
½ cup grated Cheddar cheese

In a saucepan, bring rice and water to a boil, reduce heat, and simmer rice, covered, 45 minutes, or until tender.

Heat oil in a skillet over medium heat; add beef and cook, breaking it up into small pieces with a wooden spoon. Add onion, pepper, and celery; sauté until onion is translucent. Add parsley, coriander, chili powder, cumin, beans, and broth; bring to a boil. Reduce heat and simmer stew, uncovered, 15 minutes. Add corn and simmer 5 minutes longer.

Tear tortillas into dog bite-size pieces and stir into stew. Make a bed of rice on a plate or in dog's bowl, ladle stew on top, and sprinkle with cheese. *Makes 2 quarts stew and rice.*

Pillbox

Here is a sure-fire method to get your dog to take pills with enthusiasm: Prepare a small tidbit containing the pill. While you make it, talk to your dog about the terrific treat you're about to serve. Let the dog anticipate—remember Pavlov? As he grows more eager, offer him the treat and praise him after he swallows. Dogs love to eat pills disguised in:

- cheese, including cottage, cream, and ricotta
- peanut butter—chunky works well for those clever dogs who manage to eat the goodie and spit out the pill.
- cat food—yes, it's okay to let your dog eat cat food, but *not* for your cat to eat dog food.
- white bread—the kind that compresses into a ball

BEANY LIVER CASSEROLE

Millet is a grain packed with vitamin B$_1$, a vitamin that is usually lost to heat and storage in most commercial foods. There is a theory that this vitamin contains an active agent that helps repel fleas.

8 ounces beef liver, cut into 1-inch pieces
All-purpose flour
Freshly ground black pepper
1 cup cooked kidney beans
1 onion, chopped
1 cup green beans, cut into 1-inch lengths
1 carrot, coarsely chopped
1 cup millet
3 cups Basic Dog Broth (page 83)
Bread

Preheat oven to 350° F. and grease a 2-quart casserole.

Dredge liver with flour, then sprinkle with a grinding of pepper. Place liver and kidney beans in prepared casserole. Strew onion, green beans, and carrot over liver and beans. Sprinkle millet over all and pour in enough broth to cover all ingredients. Cover casserole and bake 1 hour. Check periodically to see that liquid has not cooked away, adding broth or water as needed. Serve over chunks of bread. *Makes 1½ quarts stew.*

DAIRY PRIDE SOUP

2 onions, thinly sliced
1 parsnip, thinly sliced
1 carrot, thinly sliced
½ cup barley
2 cups Chicken Stock (page 84)
1 pound cottage cheese
½ cup corn kernels
3 cups milk
1 tablespoon tamari sauce
½ teaspoon freshly ground white pepper
½ teaspoon paprika

Place onions, parsnip, and carrot in a steamer basket and steam, covered, over boiling water 10 minutes, or until tender. Reserve.

In a saucepan, bring barley and stock to a boil over high heat. Reduce heat and cook barley, covered, 30 minutes, or until tender. Transfer barley and any liquid in saucepan to a soup kettle. Add cottage cheese, milk, tamari, and pepper. Bring mixture just to a simmer, not to a boil; add steamed vegetables. Simmer 10 minutes, or until mixture is heated through and flavors have blended. Serve in a bowl, dusted with paprika. *Makes 2½ quarts.*

Barley and cottage cheese are teamed here to provide a thick, soothing, nutritious soup, especially good fed in small amounts to a convalescing dog.

CABBAGE AND KIBBLE WITH BEEF SAUCE

The combination of cabbage, beef, and kibble results in a dish that is high in protein, fiber, and complex carbohydrates.

2 onions, thinly sliced
1 medium cabbage, chopped
1 cup peas
8 ounces lean ground beef
1 tablespoon unsalted butter (optional)
1 tablespoon all-purpose flour
1 cup Basic Dog Broth (page 83)
1 tablespoon Worcestershire sauce
Kibble (pages 73–80)

Place onions, cabbage, and peas in steamer basket and steam, covered, over boiling water 10 minutes, or until tender. Transfer vegetables to a large mixing bowl.

While vegetables are cooking, place beef in a cold skillet and cook over medium heat until crumbly, breaking up meat with a wooden spoon. Remove beef from skillet with slotted spoon and reserve. If there is very little fat left in skillet, add butter and melt over medium-low heat; stir in flour and cook, stirring constantly, until very light brown. Add broth slowly, stirring constantly, and cook over medium heat until gravy has thickened, stirring up any browned bits on bottom of skillet. Add Worcestershire sauce and cooked beef.

Add gravy to vegetables and toss to mix well. Make a small bed of kibble on a plate and spoon vegetables and gravy on top. Serve warm. *Makes 1 quart vegetable stew.*

COMMERCIAL DOG FOOD: QUALITY AND MYTHS

In *The Jungle*, published early in the twentieth century, Upton Sinclair exposed the abuses in the meat industry that had been concealed from unsuspecting consumers. Filth, contamination, and mislabeling were rampant. As a result, the Federal Meat Inspection Act was passed in 1906. Today we have government controls in the meat industry, but their effectiveness is under scrutiny.

Most of us have never taken a tour of a slaughterhouse and thus are blissfully unaware of how those animals herded into the holding pens in the processing center are transformed into the the sanitized, packaged squares of meat you see when you cruise through the meat section of your supermarket.

In 1985 and 1987 the National Academy of Sciences (NAS), a private advisory group to the federal government, condemned the slaughterhouse inspection of meat and poultry as inadequate, calling for a new poultry inspection system altogether. Overworked inspectors of the United States Department of Agriculture (USDA) have only a few seconds to inspect each carcass for at least twenty different potential problems.

Bribery and extortion charges continue to plague inspectors and plant owners.

There is, of course, some attempt to control the quality of meat that is graded and approved for human consumption. However, despite Federal Drug Administration (FDA) efforts, the educated consumer knows that there are many suspect practices in the meat industry.

Antibiotics. During their short lifetimes, animals are fed huge quantities of antibiotics to prevent disease that could result from overcrowding. In fact, half of all the antibiotics manufactured in the United States are fed to livestock.

The FDA has been investigating the health effects of antibiotics on food animals since 1972. In 1977 the agency proposed a ban on penicillin and tetracycline in all animal feed. The proposal stalled in Congress, which asked for more studies.

In 1987, the Center for Disease Control documented the second major outbreak of antibiotic-resistant salmonella in three years. No action has yet been taken, although the FDA is requesting more studies.

Other chemicals. Animals bred for human consumption are fed grains that have been subject to chemical fertilizers and pesticides. Animals are also fed growth hormones to increase their size. And we know that sometimes all the red meat in the market looks freshly dipped in red food coloring to simulate freshness.

Even with government standards and inspection, the picture is chilling because, as we also know, we are what we eat.

For our pets it's even worse. Dogs and cats get the

leftovers at the meat packers. Meat and poultry for human consumption is inspected by the USDA, in however cursory a manner, but while some states regulate pet food canning processes, it is not mandated at the federal level.

In pet food it is not illegal to include what is commonly called "4-D" meat. The Ds stand for the condition of the animal as it arrives at the slaughterhouse—diseased, disabled, dying, or dead. According to the FDA, this practice is acceptable since, during the rendering process, the meat is subject to very high temperatures to kill any bacteria or virus.

However, the checks on the manufacturers are at best haphazard. They fit under the GMP ("good manufacturing process") guidelines, which mean that the pet food manufacturers are required only to file a form informing the FDA of the processing method. On-site investigations are rare, occurring only when there is a "for cause" basis.

Is it any wonder that you turn green every time you open a can of dog food and get a whiff of its contents?

In addition to the FDA, there are two other agencies that regulate requirements and labeling practices. The first, the National Research Council (NRC), part of the National Academy of Sciences, has since 1962 determined the nutritional requirements for pets (as well as for humans) and has set minimum levels for nutrients required by dogs. The standard requires that the food will enable the pet to grow to normal size, maintain normal weight as an adult, and enable fertility, gestation, and lactation.

In 1985 the NRC Subcommittee on Dog Nutrition, chaired by Dr. Ben E. Sheffy of Cornell University, upgraded its requirements. The 1974 standards prompted many dog food manufacturers to include the phrase "meets or exceeds NRC requirements" on their packaging on the sole basis of chemical analysis.

According to Dr. Sheffy, it is no longer sufficient to state what is in the food if it is not available nutritionally to the dog. Many dog food manufacturers resist the expensive tests necessary to measure how much of the nutrients are retained and how much are lost. As a result, a consumer may be deceived by the phrase "meets or exceeds NRC requirements" which refers to the old standard based on chemical analysis, not the availability of the nutrients to the dog.

Under the new guidelines, the caloric value of food is measured per 1,000 calories per pound of energy (digestible calories, which is more accurate than caloric value measured simply per pound of food. Dr. Sheffy believes that within a short time, manufacturers will be required to state the number of digestible calories per unit of food.

The second agency, the American Association of Feed Control Officials (AAFCO) is made up of 200 members who are officials of agencies that regulate the manufacture, sale, and distribution of animal food. AAFCO tests pet food, promotes uniformity in definitions that appear on pet food labels, and assists in ruling on and in the enforcement of the laws. AAFCO analyzes pet foods continually to ensure that the ingredients in the package are consistent with the analysis on the label.

As more research is compiled on dog nutrition, AAFCO test protocols have become more strict. In order for a dog food to pass their tests, the mature offspring of bitches that have been fed an exclusive diet of the test food must conform to growth curves and certain blood values before the food is rated acceptable.

Veterinarians have long recognized the necessity of sound animal nutrition. The American Veterinary Medical Association and the Small Animal Hospitals Association are proposing a certification program to improve animal nutrition. These groups would like to undertake plant inspection and formula analysis, which will cost the manufacturer about three-quarters of a cent for every pound of food that is sold.

Some of the major dog food manufacturers are now underwriting the necessary testing, and it is hoped that others will follow. If you are going to use a commercial dog food, read the labels carefully and select one that conforms to the 1985 NRC and AAFCO standards.

On all commercial dog food labels, be sure to read the fine print following the main ingredients—those multisyllable, chemical-sounding names and letters. These are the additives. Many veterinary nutrition experts believe that some of these substances decrease pet health.

Dry foods. Kibbled brands you might want to use include, in alphabetical order, Bench and Field, Cornucopia, Eukanuba, Haute Canine, Hi-Tor, Hill's, Iams, Purina O.N.E., Purina Pro, Triumph, Wayne's, and Wysong.

Brands that use natural preservatives (vitamins C and E, or ethoxyquin) instead of the controversial BHA include A.N.F., Bench and Field, Cornucopia, Hi-Tor, and Purina O.N.E.

Canned food. For an interesting comparison, take your calculator with you the next time you go to the supermarket. Compare the price per pound of ground beef at the meat counter with the price per pound of any of the canned dog food brands—from the most expensive to the least. In my own investigation, at the low end, supermarket-brand canned dog dinner was six times cheaper than the packaged hamburger at the butcher's counter.

Then ask yourself: If this dog food—after processing, canning, marketing, distribution, and advertising—costs six times *less* than ground meat, how can it possibly be everything the advertisers claim?

Most canned dog food isn't all meat, nor should it be. Fillers are used in wet, dry, and semi-moist food, and in canned foods the fillers may be rice, barley, corn, meat byproducts, meals, powders, additives, and water. The FDA applies to pet foods labeling standards that are similar to those for human food.

- "beef stew" must be 25 percent beef
- "beef dinner" must contain between 25 and 95 percent beef
- "beef" alone should contain 95 percent beef
- "all beef" means that the can should contain only beef, and therefore it cannot be fortified with added vitamins.
- "beef flavor" means there must be enough beef present to impart a beef taste

If you've been searching for high-quality canned food for your dog, Carnation's Mighty Dog is an excellent canned food that meets federal standards for human consumption. Hill's Science Diet is another nutritious canned dog food, and in addition, Hill's offers a full line of prescription canned dog foods for special needs.

Semimoist food. Plastic-wrapped "burgers" are very popular. They look a little like the real thing, but they require no cooking and don't smell offensive. Something you notice immediately is the rubber, synthetic quality and unnatural coloring. But it's the sugar that we should be concerned about, since most semimoist dog foods require over 20 percent sugar to bind them. Obviously, the semimoist burgers aren't for the diabetic dog; but even for the normal dog, this excess of sugar will deplete the body's stores of vitamins and minerals. The advantage of using semimoist "burgers" is their convenience, especially when you and your pet are traveling, but they are not recommended as a daily dog food diet.

In closing, although there are indeed nutritionally adequate commercial dog foods, nothing can compare with the food you prepare yourself. Your dog's enjoyment of food will soar to new heights as he learns to savor tastes and textures unknown in commercial dog foods.

When you use only the freshest ingredients, you can feel confident that you're making a significant contribution to your pet's vigor and *joie de vivre* at the same time that you're keeping his meals free of additives, contaminants, or over-processed foods. Now your dog's mealtime can be an eagerly anticipated event for both of you.

Bone Appétit!

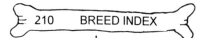

Breed Index

This page is dedicated to the memory of our beloved pet, Marvin, a "plain brown dog." Marvin was a retriever, terrier, shepherd mix who inherited the best traits of all his ancestors.